REMEMBER TO FORGET

a journey out of denial, repressed memories and defilement - into truth, freedom and worth.
by Sarah Hemli

WestBow Press books may be ordered through booksellers or by contacting:

WestBow Press
A Division of Thomas Nelson & Zondervan
1663 Liberty Drive
Bloomington, IN 47403
www.westbowpress.com
1 (866) 928-1240

Interior and Cover Layouts by Sarah Hemli.

ISBN: 978-1-5127-3227-6 (sc)
ISBN: 978-1-5127-3226-9 (e)

Library of Congress Control Number: 2016902944

Print information available on the last page.

WestBow Press rev. date: 3/1/2016

WESTBOW
PRESS®
A DIVISION OF THOMAS NELSON
& ZONDERVAN

TABLE OF CONTENTS

FOREWORD
by Dahlia

When I first had the privilege of reading this book, I could not put it down. I felt like I was reading something sacred and profound. I kept thinking of all the women and men who needed to read it because they were also hurting and needed to know that they could also make it.

This is not your typical read for those who have struggled with the trauma of sexual abuse. This is gut wrenching and raw. By using her real words and her honest struggle seen clearly in her emails, Sarah takes the reader on a journey through incredible pain and suffering. There were times that I did not know if she would make it. The pictures that she drew representing what she could not say moved me to tears. The juxtaposition of the words and the drawings gave me such a rich picture of what she was thinking and feeling as she struggled to make sense of what had happened to her and whether there would ever be healing.

I remember the first day I met Sarah. A friend asked me if I would consider talking to someone that he had been coaching. He thought she needed more than he could offer her. I agreed to just talk to her on the phone so that she could meet me and I could get a sense of what to recommend for her. But as the day approached, I wasn't sure that the call would even take place. My friend said that he would be on the phone too so that she would have some semblance of safety-it is incredibly scary to talk to someone you do not know about the deepest things that you have never told.

In order to survive, Sarah had created stories about her childhood that seemed better than the story she was trying to forget. She denied and minimized what happened and made it her fault. She told herself that she had made it all up. She had been accused of that. What if I did not believe her? Everything in her was screaming for her to run! I didn't know then what I know now, that the phone call took such incredible courage and determination to get well.

Sarah made that same brave choice over and over again as she reentered the confusion and pain of her abusive childhood that she had tried so hard to forget. And nothing was the same after that. The vast majority was positive but there were some painful costs to facing the truth, some that could not be undone.

Looking back, I cannot believe the transformation that has happened in Sarah. From a woman who did not know that she could have a voice, to an incredibly strong woman who has such a deep, compassionate, powerful and creative voice. I have so much admiration for the woman that Sarah is. It has been a privilege to get to walk alongside her as she has taken such courageous steps in her own healing. Her journey would take her from the God of her father to the God of her heart.

I am so thankful that I agreed to talk to Sarah that day. My life has been so immensely blessed by knowing her. She has taught me much about perseverance, honesty, hope and courage as she has chosen day after day to keep fighting for her own healing. I will forever be grateful.

Some roads you can only walk
if the right people are walking with you.

LEAVING PERFECT
CHILDHOOD LAND

I was so nervous. I walked around the house restless, not really present. Why did I agree to this? What was I thinking? I agreed to it a long time ago when friends were visiting from Denmark. They noticed the struggles between my husband and me and between us and the six special-needs foster kids in our household at the time. My friends thought it would be good to have "Aaron" come and help us learn better communication, better ways to handle stress.

"Life Coach" was his title. Amazing, kind, gentle, helpful, and caring were the words one of my friends used to describe him. The list went on. My friend clearly had a close relationship with this man. "I know you need help, Sarah. I'm sending you the best help I know." I trusted my friend. I agreed to it, but

it had "DANGER" written all over it.

Now the day had come when Aaron would arrive. Bruce, my husband, had gone to the airport to pick him up. I kept telling myself we'd talk about the kids, talk about Bruce and his issues, talk about better ways to communicate. **No reason to ever talk about me**.

But somewhere deep inside was a tiny **seed of hope** — hope, or maybe just a fantasy, that someday somehow someone would care enough to make it to the truth, to help me discover what was lost.

I never talked about me— the real me. Sure

I'd tell stories and share superficial stuff. I knew lots of funny stories from my past. I didn't talk about me. It felt unsafe. I had a few people close to me, but not close enough to make me vulnerable. I had always had a sense that if people really knew me, **if I let them see who I actually was**, they would be **disgusted**. They would never speak to me again or ever want to be around me. People thought they knew me, but if someone ever came too close, I'd push them away by ending the relationship.

This was true of regular people—friends. When it came to doctors, teacher, pastors, and, worst of all, therapists and counsellors, **extreme caution was necessary and no trust given.**

Here I was, seeing the car pull into the driveway and a man getting out. Warning signals were going off: "Life coach… RUN, run now while you can."

I **put on my smile** and greeted him. The three of us chatted for a few minutes. I

Sarah Hemli

slightly hid behind Bruce and let him do the talking. I smiled, laughed, and nodded at the appropriate times. Aaron needed something to eat, and then he said, "Let's get started."

Waves of fear rolled over me. I hoped no one noticed me shaking.

We sat down, and Aaron began talking to Bruce. His first question was, "**Tell me about your upbringing**." I felt light headed. If he had asked me that question, I could have potentially throw up on my white carpet.

Twenty minutes later a startling reality hit me—Bruce had to go pick up one of our kids.

Before I knew it, I was sitting alone with Aaron. It wasn't his first question; it was his fourth. I don't remember the first three, and I don't remember how he actually asked it, but I do remember everything in me screaming

"LIE, LIE! DO NOT TELL!" Then out of my mouth came, "I don't remember my childhood."

Time stood still. All my inner alarm bells went off. My mind went down the list of explanations as to why I didn't remember. Abuse and trauma were not on the list!

Over fifteen years ago, I made drawings of me standing in a room by a little round door in a wall. I forgot about them. Well, I wanted to forget about them. They were made in some of my most **honest and brave moments**. I claimed then I had no idea what they were about. All I knew was that something was **hidden, inaccessible**—not to ever come out. I made these very specific comments then:

Dark, cold and moist - bare stone wall
only I am there and the little door. I have to keep guard so nothing leaks from the door.
I've never been in there, but my sense is it's a big rectangle room.
I don't know what is in there, I just know that it can't come out.

I think this room is without a ceiling - at least not stone. I think it's open to a big dark sky. Maybe I fell in here. The walls are high, impossible to get out that way. The little door is right at my stomach.

It's hard to breathe, I'm scared, sad, alone, painful. I don't want to leave here, I have to do something first. Or I'm scared to leave the door, it might leak.

Sarah Hemli

My life turned upside down the moment I admitted to Aaron that I didn't remember my childhood. The admission was a huge step for me. It contained so much. In that moment, I felt completely exposed. I had lost control.

I had invited someone else into that space by the little door to the room holding the ugly unknown.

I had no idea what would happen in the next four days and beyond. I had opened a door for Aaron to see, that is if he cared enough to go there with me.

I don't remember much of our conversations from the four days Aaron was with us. My body reacted. It got cold and shaky as we spoke. I was **overwhelmed, scared, and in disbelief.** But I felt heard and seen in a way that I had never felt before. Not that people in my life refused to hear and see me, I had just never let them.

Although fear and disbelief were strong, there was a **subtle sense of relief.** I had lived for so many years not noticing how heavy this burden was. It was normalcy to me. I had accepted that it was just part of me. The burden was mine to carry.

Could it be that I didn't have to live this way?

For the first time in a long time, **I felt God close.** I knew He was behind all this.

At the same time, I tried to wake myself up from this madness. Really, this was crazy! I knew about my past.

I had a good childhood, a happy one. I was a **little girl full of joy**, invention, and imagination. I was a handful, always busy testing boundaries.

I grew up in Denmark with both of my parents and my three-years-older brother.

We moved the first time when I was almost two. This was a move to a new town where my parents were involved in planting a church. We lived in the same house until I was twelve, when we moved a block away to a bigger house. My aunt moved in with us.

In addition to being an unpaid pastor, my dad was an engineer and worked different jobs. My mom ran a daycare in our house when I was younger, then worked at a daycare center when I was older. My brother was quiet, not very social, but very smart and well-behaved.

When he was little, he kept his toys on the shelves. He'd play with one at a time, and then put it back. As soon as I could crawl,

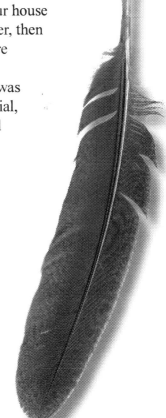

everything was on the floor.

There were several stories of how opposite we were. Stories of the quiet, older brother and the rambunctious, little sister.

I don't know if it was ever directly said, but when two children are so opposite and one is intelligent, obedient, smart, talented and good... well, it's pretty **obvious what the other child is.**

The one story that I disliked the most was one my mom would tell of how they had my brother and thought they'd have many kids, but then they had me and decided they were done having kids.

This was my reality. This was my past. Except for a handful of fuzzy memories, I only knew what had been told to me.

My mom did an excellent job with photo albums. I have album after album with photos of every Christmas, New Year, birthday, Easter, visit with Grandma and Grandpa, beginning of a new grade, family party, and everyday moments.

I don't know how many times, I'd thought I had remembered something from my past, only to find that it was a photo of a situation that I remembered.

Through my education in human development, early childhood, and special needs, I had learned it wasn't normal to have **no memories**, but I didn't make a big deal out of it. **"I just don't have a good memory,"** I told myself.

I lived my life, grew up, studied, and got jobs. I was good at what I did. I was well-liked. I had times in my life when I almost forgot the burden. Things were working out for me. I always kept very busy with a full life.

Then there was a sense that

something was not right.

A sense that I always had but denied. I held on tight to the story of a happy childhood, but in my most honest moments, I would admit there was **something hidden, forgotten, and buried deep in me**. Something that should never see the light of day. Something that would destroy me if I let it surface.

I was very aware of people. I had to keep them at a distance. At the same time, a part of me so desperately wanted to be seen and known— the scared, lonely, honest part of me.

But I played it safe. Stay hidden and keep people at a safe distance. **I knew for a fact that if anyone really knew me they would abandon me.**

Now I let Aaron closer than anyone had ever been. I was **more honest than I'd ever been.** As I talked about how I felt about myself, Aaron said the word

"defilement."

I claimed I didn't know what the word

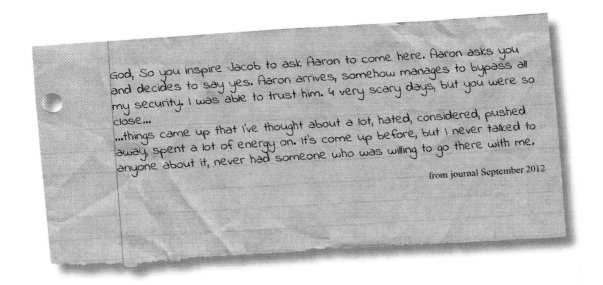

God, So you inspire Jacob to ask Aaron to come here. Aaron asks you and decides to say yes. Aaron arrives, somehow manages to bypass all my security. I was able to trust him. 4 very scary days, but you were so close...

...things came up that I've thought about a lot, hated, considered, pushed away, spent a lot of energy on. It's come up before, but I never talked to anyone about it, never had someone who was willing to go there with me.

from journal September 2012

meant. Though I might not have been completely sure, it **resonated deep in me**.

I was defiled. I was a horrible person. **I did unforgivable things,** and I should suffer forever. I deserved the worst. I deserved punishment and pain. I wasn't worthy of love or care. Not people's love. Not God's love!

Several **images** came to mind while talking and praying with Aaron. Aaron **never proposed anything**. He never suggested or gave me his conclusions. He simply **asked God** to show me what He wanted to.

Growing up in a church environment, I experienced so many words spoken over me, prophecies given, prayers prayed for me—

all with the **authority of God, but originating in a human mind** and forced on me. So this worked for me.

It seemed quite risky to allow an

unpredictable God to communicate and do what he wanted to, but I'd rather that than have God talk to me through a human mind.

My mind is very visual so I was just fine with images. Most of the images I saw were beautiful and full of promise. It was God showing me He felt differently about me than I had ever imagined. He loved me. He rejoiced in me. **He came to meet me** where I was.

Early Sunday morning me and Father.

Sarah Hemli

One image was hard to swallow.

That morning in the shower I had asked God to just show me **when and where** it happened. That was all I could handle for the time being.

As an adult I had never been able to remember what my childhood bedroom looked like. I could picture the hallway and I knew the layout of the house, but as I "opened" the door to **my room** it was **all white fog**.

Now I saw this image of my childhood bedroom. I saw my **pale blue toddler bed** passed down from my brother. It was decorated with stickers my brother had put on there and my mom had tried unsuccessfully to remove. I saw the white dots on my red comforter. I saw the little pictures on the wall. I **heard the clicky sound** of the handles on my dresser drawers, and I saw my doll house on top of the dresser.

When and where? **My mind was racing.** My toddler bed? What? I would have been so little and in my bedroom, who could have gotten to me there?

But then the rest of the image got my attention. There in the middle of the room sitting on the floor leaning up against my bed was a **large being,** kind of curled up and **crying**.

It took a little time before I realized who this was. **God was there.** He was in the "when" and the "where." **He was crying**.

That was the last day Aaron was with us. After Aaron left to go home, **I lost it.** We were joking about it. "I really need to have serious conversations with my security people, because Aaron just went straight through all security checkpoints." I laughed, but really I was terrified.

I DO NOT TRUST PEOPLE! What happened? I let him into my most secret place just like that. I had pushed people away for much less than that, and I certainly had to **get Aaron to go away.**

I don't know if I ever sent the email telling him we had enough of his help. I think Bruce did.

It just can't be true! I've realized that I just can't do it. I can't accept it, I can't live with it. It's too devastating. I don't know what to do. I have to find a way to get back to where I was before you came, I'm so sorry. I don't want you to waste any more time on this – or your friend's time in North Carolina. I'm so sorry, I wish I had never agreed for you to come, you could have spent your week helping people who really need it. You are an amazing man, your compassion and care is overwhelming. I'm sorry, I don't know how to say sorry enough.

email to Aaron September 2012

Aaron didn't accept the boot. He wasn't disgusted. He didn't run for the hills.

He wouldn't go away.

The following days were hard. I felt torn. I desperately wanted to **forget everything** that had just happened and return to normal. It seemed safer to carry everything in secret. I was **beating myself up** for ever agreeing to Aaron coming to see us. How I wished I had never said yes.

On the other hand, I was **relieved** to not have to carry this burden alone anymore. And I had a sense God was doing something. If God was on the move, would I really **want to fight Him?**

I'm beginning to feel like I'm getting back control. Last week was so intense and now I've had time to think about it. I've been able to button things up a bit, everything was so raw and emotional. The fact is that I don't remember, it's just not there, so how could anything have happened?! And who could have done it?! It just doesn't make sense. I have a bad recollection in general, maybe I don't remember my childhood cos there was nothing significant to remember. I really just want to go back to how things were before. I can try harder and make things work between Bruce and I. I can try harder to lose weight and become pretty. I can try harder at sex, not turn him down so much, not take the porn so seriously. And my weird issues about certain things freaking me out during sex, I will have to find a way to get over them. I guess I need to be less opinionated... hmm, probably in many things.
We need to work on communication. It hasn't been a problem this past week. Bruce is a lot different. He doesn't want sex, he wants me, not my body, but me! That's amazing. He pulls my PJ shirt down to cover my skin, he use to pull it up and I would try to fend him off. So different, but probably just for a time. I wonder if he still wants me now that he thinks he knows what I did a long time ago.

I know that I said that I'm convinced something did happen. It just somehow gave me hope that things can be better, that this burden could be gone. It just explains so much for me. The panic I feel in certain intimate situations, my hate for my body, my bad choices in the past, my lack of trust toward people, my need for control... Man, I fit so many things on that checklist, I don't want to go back to look. Some of them are kind of sick, I don't want to fit them. I'm sure there could be many reasons for my weirdness, it doesn't have to be this.
What about my fantasy world when I was a teenager? Just a low self esteem, confused pastor's kid. I remember wanting people to notice me, I so desperately wanted someone to understand me, tell me what was wrong with me and fix me. So I made up stuff to be interesting, to be noticed, to get attention. It never worked, nobody really got me, I didn't.
I didn't. There's always been something, always been the sense of something. Maybe I just wanted there to be something. Perfect childhood, happily married parents, good home - all that stuff. Maybe I just want there to be something, perfect is not interesting!

part of email to Aaron October 2012

the fear of what might happen

Sarah Hemli

The fear of letting go was quite overwhelming.

Searching the web, I found a **list of possible issues** that one might deal with as a result of abuse. I **freaked out** when I read on the list behavior I had thought was normal.

It was beyond **difficult to admit**: I had been **abused** years ago. But I was relieved to connect the feelings of

shame, defilement, disgust, and hate

to their origin.

At that point, I understood where and when, but I still had no memories of how or who.

WHO?

That was the scariest question for me. I did not

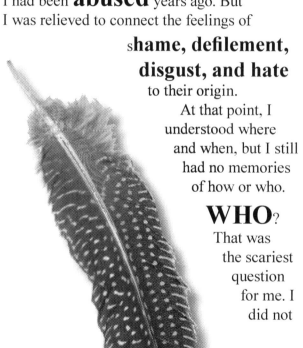

remember, but really - I knew.

Ten years ago, when I was still living in Denmark, **images surfaced in my mind** that pulled the rug out from under me. Images of playing and swinging on the swing set in the yard, **my dad's hands touching my very young body.**

At the time, I saw my parents often. The images had to be false memories. **My dad's a man of God.** He would never do such a thing. I struggled for a time then finally concluded the images were f**alse memories or an attack from the enemy.** Since then, I kept the images buried, hidden from consciousness, away from reality.

There were more inklings, situations that baffled me. The time in my late teens that, our friends' two little girls gladly told me my dad played with them. **I completely panicked.** Something in me knew that was a really bad thing.

When I was thirteen, I wrote a novel about a young girl who had a very difficult life and was raped several times.

Later in life there were the times when I was visiting my parents and changing in my room, I forgot to close the door all the way. I had a sense that my dad was in the hallway watching me.

I'd tell myself they were **crazy**

Sarah Hemli

thoughts and it was all in my head. It was ridiculous. **Not my dad and not me.**

I fought hard to deny what I knew was true. But I couldn't turn back. My journey had begun, and I **couldn't go back to perfect childhood-land**. I was **headed for reality.**

I was **in over my head** and I knew it. I needed help, whether or not I had the guts to admit what I knew to be true. Whatever was behind the door wanted out. Facing it alone would **surely kill me**. Still I wasn't ready to step out and seek help. I chose denial.

Denial was a beautiful thing. It enabled me to keep on going in spite of knowing the truth. I held to the fact that I still had **no actual memories** of abuse. But I knew that the story of my upbringing was a made up one.

Yes, there were happy, beautiful, and photographic times. It wasn't all bad. But in **between those happy snapshots**

was agony.

I had completely shut off a large part of me, as if it didn't exist, but it still had power over my life and my choices. In me was a **lost, little girl** who had endured so much but **who had no voice** and no acceptance.

I'm not sure how I came up with the idea to write a letter to my former self, the lost, little girl, but **it made sense in my heart.**

Writing the letter soothed the commotion on the inside of me, but I was unprepared for the memories it would release. What was I asking for in this letter? Three days later, I wrote a second letter.

Dear Little girl,
It wasn't your fault. You were only a small child, you didn't know what to do. The grownups around you should have taken better care of you, it shouldn't have happened, it wasn't your fault.
I blame you for nothing!
I haven't been taking very good care of you either. I've pushed you away hid you, I've not allowed you to live.
Forgive me that I forgot about you. Forgive me for eating to cover you up. Forgive me that I'd rather deny that you exist. Forgive me that I have not given you room until now.
You were just a little girl, they should have cared for you. It shouldn't have happened.
Little girl, I'll take care of it now, you can let go, let it out. Don't be afraid anymore, you have the right to exist.
Everything that happened - none of it was your fault. You gave up, the struggle was so overwhelming there was nothing you could do, what did you know?
Try to trust me now, show me everything, let it come into the light so it can lose it's power over you. You will find peace and joy. I know it's hard to let go, I will take care of it, I promise.
Please for me and for you - show me. Show me your room, show me your face, show me the pain and the fear, show me what happened, show me who.
It's ok, I won't be angry. Nobody can hurt you anymore, I'll take care of you now.
Little girl, can you trust me? I have not been there for you for so many years, I've let you down, I know, but I'm here now.
Sarah

November 1st 2012, translated from danish

Sarah Hemli

Dear little girl,

I think I've seen you in a "dream". It began with that time you were climbing on the outside of the railing around the end of your road. It was always fun and you never fell, but it was not allowed – actually it was quite dangerous.

That day you dad caught you. I don't know if you walked or he carried you. But he took you to his bedroom and you got a spanking. For so many years I've remembered that and I've always hated spanking.

In the dream I saw what happened after. I saw his hand not hitting you anymore, but moving over your bottom and...

... You were laying there very still. Was all that just a dream or did that really happen? I can't see your face or his face.

You know, little girl, that's not actually part of a spanking...

The other dream is not connected to something I remember. First I see the view from laying on the end of the bed. If you look up you see the window and the gray clouds outside. If you look to the right you see the back of the desk. I can see details of things on the desk and the books and binders on the shelf under the desk. I remember how you cleaned that up in your head...

After that I see everything as if I'm hanging in the ceiling. I see you enter the room, your dad is sitting on his chair by his desk, he calls you 'Fars pige' (dad's girl).

...later I see you on the end of the bed, I see the view of the clouds and the back of the desk. You are naked...

...Doesn't it hurt? You are just laying there with your arms down by your side looking at the back of the desk...

...I see your flat chest, you are not very old. It's not at all ok , you were not old enough to have sex. But you don't make a sound, you are so still. Have you given up? I can understand if you did, it must have been so overwhelming and painful, I can't even imagine.

I will take care of it, I promise.

Sarah

November 3rd 2012, translated from danish.

Memories of my childhood came flooding back. The first memories were **absolutely overwhelming** — okay, every single memory was overwhelming, but the first ones were **unreal**. As soon as a memory showed up, an army of theories and explanations followed to **disarm and invalidate** it entirely. It was exhausting to sort through the long list of reasons it could not be actual memories.

To begin with it was like **watching a bad movie,** I was detached from the situation. I was not the little girl on the bed, rather I stood apart for the situation. As she looked around the room, I began to

remember details from her perspective. But then he would interact with her, and I was again outside looking in.

It was **unreal**, yet so **familiar**. I felt crazy for writing letters to my younger self. I needed to care for her, to make sure she was alright. She was my ally. I had to take care of her to understand what really happened. **Only she and my dad knew the truth.**

Aaron claimed he was not qualified to help me work through my past. That was okay; **I wasn't planning to work through it** anyway. He knew someone qualified. Good for him, but that had nothing to do with me, since **I wasn't sharing this with another person**, ever. Aaron spoke very highly of a therapist, **Dahlia**, but I wasn't impressed. I wanted Aaron to be the only other person in the world who would ever know my secret. **The shame was heavy.** Having Aaron know was already one person too many. I had already ruled out talking to a local counselor. The therapist pool in our small, Midwest community is limited, and I knew most of them from working with our foster kids.

Somehow I agreed to have a three way conversation over the phone with Dahlia, who practiced in a different state. I was nervous

Sarah Hemli

for days. Hours before the phone call **I was panicking**. It was the diarrhea, cold sweat and shaking -kind of anticipation.

The first thing Dahlia said was, "Sarah, so nice to meet you." I thought, "Yeah, not a mutual feeling, lady."

But there was something about her that **made me feel calm and safe.** It was odd, since I knew therapists were not safe. She could potentially **unravel my denial.** But maybe she could see my pain. Maybe she knew exactly what I was talking about. Maybe it all made sense to her. Maybe she would be willing to walk with me through the deepest pain and scariest memories. **Maybe, just maybe, she would be safe.**

Until this point, I had made it too **difficult for people to reach me**, but I wanted nothing more than for someone to care enough about me to get through my defenses, although it **frightened** me.

After meeting Dahlia on the phone and telling her part my story, she agreed to work with me, but she wouldn't do therapy over the phone. She suggested I travel to North Carolina for a week of **intensive therapy**. I had to do it. I told myself that this would be the way to prove the movies in my head wrong. I needed someone with her experience to tell me I had false memories. I had to know for sure they were all made up. I **needed to know what was really wrong with me.**

Honestly, it was too much to carry the burden of shame by myself. I needed help. **I needed to trust somebody.**

I decided to go to North Carolina, and I called Dahlia to tell her we're on. She said great, but then told me I needed to find someone to go with me. I didn't want anyone else there, so I backed out. Aaron and his wife Grace offered to go, but **I was unmoved**. I didn't know how to receive that kind of care.

Sarah Hemli

I was a mess. I desperately tried to explain and **deny** and **forget**.

I talked to Dahlia over the phone a few more times, then I finally decided to go see her for **a week of intensive therapy**. Aaron and Grace met me there and spend the week taking care of me. At the time, I thought **they were crazy** to travel so far and so long just to support me, hang out with me, cook for me, and drive me back and forth from Dahlia's office. They were **part of a bigger picture** I couldn't see at the time. Aaron and Grace were exactly what I needed.

It turns out they were not crazy; **they just decided to love me.**

Aaron,
I can't do this. Dahlia is not available until January, that is so far away and that's when my parents are gonna be back. I'm not gonna make it that far, even if I did - Bruce is gonna kick me out before then. I understand that he called you this afternoon - I do not want Sofia to go with me to North Carolina or where ever. I'm not going. Bruce is not gonna be satisfied until I tell all of our friends what a pervert I am. I'm done.

part of email to Aaron November 2012

Actually, I've done pretty good for many days up until a few days ago. I've managed to push everything away and focus on other things. We even had people over and I did a good job being cute and happy and chatty. But then it all came rushing back, I got a couple of new movies I had to deal with. And an old one that I had counted as not possible because I knew we didn't have a bathroom downstairs, turns out we did. It was really overwhelming and no amount of food or wine would make it go away.
So I made up a new theory of my movies - I'm subconsciously making them up to explain my strong dislikes about certain things. Like my Dad has these fabric handkerchiefs that he carries around. I've never thought much about it, I just don't like them. To this day, I will not take one from him to use for anything regardless of how 'just washed' it is or even out of a new pack. I can't stand them. There was a handkerchief in one of the new movies. Could that be it? What does that make me? A pervert?
Coming up with these theories to prove everything wrong helps a little bit, but it also hurts. It mostly hurts, really, now that I think about it.

part of email to Gary December 2012

Sarah Hemli

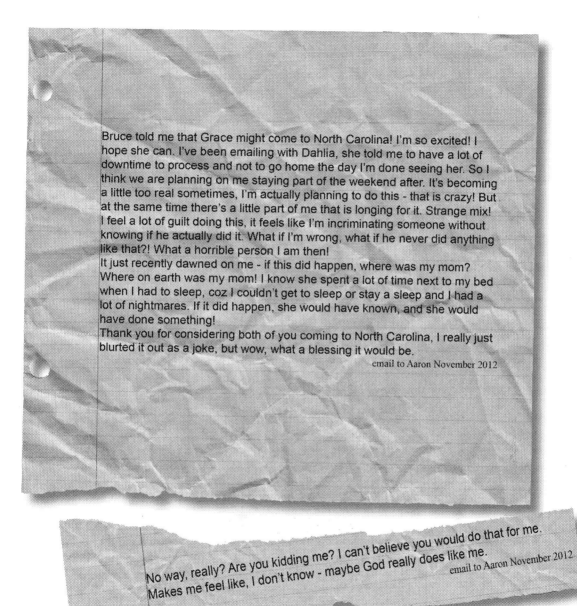

Bruce told me that Grace might come to North Carolina! I'm so excited! I hope she can. I've been emailing with Dahlia, she told me to have a lot of downtime to process and not to go home the day I'm done seeing her. So I think we are planning on me staying part of the weekend after. It's becoming a little too real sometimes, I'm actually planning to do this - that is crazy! But at the same time there's a little part of me that is longing for it. Strange mix! I feel a lot of guilt doing this, it feels like I'm incriminating someone without knowing if he actually did it. What if I'm wrong, what if he never did anything like that?! What a horrible person I am then!

It just recently dawned on me - if this did happen, where was my mom? Where on earth was my mom! I know she spent a lot of time next to my bed when I had to sleep, coz I couldn't get to sleep or stay a sleep and I had a lot of nightmares. If it did happen, she would have known, and she would have done something!

Thank you for considering both of you coming to North Carolina, I really just blurted it out as a joke, but wow, what a blessing it would be.

email to Aaron November 2012

No way, really? Are you kidding me? I can't believe you would do that for me. Makes me feel like, I don't know - maybe God really does like me.

email to Aaron November 2012

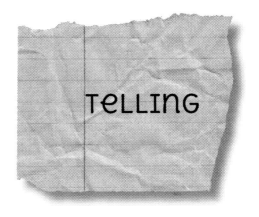

TELLING

I didn't sleep much the night before

meeting Dahlia. I had spoken to
her over the phone, but now she would be a
body and I would too. She would see me, look
in my eyes. Would she see me shaking? Would
she see my fear?

Aaron took me to her office building. I
went straight to the restroom and hid for a
while. Then I walked in circles in the hallway.

What was I doing? **How did I get myself into this?**

It felt like my mind tried to swim up
a waterfall to get back to a place where
everything was hidden again. Where the
reality of my past was only photos in an
album. How could I ever get back there? What
I was about to do seemed like the **last step before no turning back**.

I sat on the edge of the couch as close to
the door as possible. I had planned my escape
if it would become necessary. I studied the
room, I studied her. Who has that many books
about sex on their shelves?

Forty-five minutes into the conversation,
Dahlia kindly suggested for me to get more
comfortable.

I discarded the escape plan and decided that
Dahlia was **safe**. Mostly
because **I needed her to be.**

The first day with Dahlia wasn't so bad.
We talked about other aspects of my life. No
childhood memories. I was **completely exhausted**, but probably because of how
nervous I was.

I walked away from her office with
overwhelming homework. I had to draw
pictures to represent each memory. I had
already written down most of the memories
as letters to the little girl. The letters were in
Danish since she wouldn't have known English
at the time and so that nobody in my current
world would be able to know what horrible
stories I had written down.

That evening I made little **drawings to each memory**. It was **awful**. All
the drawings were symbolic, not a single one
of an actual situation. I gave validity to what
I wanted to be untrue, made up, imagination,
mental sickness, crazy. It was awful and scary
to let it out even like that. **I would take anything over reality.**

I slept little that night, but still managed to
get up and off to see Dahlia. As I was walking
up the stairs to her office, I thought, "If only
I could sink

Sarah Hemli

into the staircase and disappear." It was **one of the hardest days of my life.**

When I finally let out what I was supposed to keep hidden, I was overwhelmed by strong and not quite rational emotions. I **panicked**.

I told! It was so ingrained in me how bad telling would be, how my world would end if I told. I was gripped by fear, and no amount of common sense made a difference. I told the unthinkable. **I told the truth**.

To my surprise, Dahlia didn't run. She

Today was horrible, I've never had such a hard time sharing anything. My deepest and worst is out there, it's scary!
When we first began talking I thought – ok, there's no way I can do this, I cannot get those words across my lips. I had trouble writing them in danish to the little girl who already knows it all, but to tell someone in the present world was just horrific. I will never tell another person again in my life. Nobody else will ever know.
I was almost afraid to carry it with me out in the world. What if it really happened? I wonna hide from the world. I hope Bruce doesn't call. I can't believe I let it out. Well, I can't believe I ever let Aaron come to our home, I can't believe I didn't lie when he asked about my childhood. I can't believe I came here. What was I thinking, all this was never suppose to see the light of day. But Dahlia knows now, what is she gonna do with it? What does she think?
I feel like hiding, I've been exposed, but I did it. The one thing that I was to never tell anybody, I told! What am I gonna do?
I never want to see that little girl again, I hate her. She should have done better, she should have fought. She should have told. Why didn't she tell, she could have stopped it. I hate her. How am I never gonna show her grace?!

from journal January 2013

Cried myself to sleep - woke up in a puddle, so sad. Flashes of spank-
ings and touching.
I did not want to see Heath ever again, she has way too much information
about me. I did consider other options like jumping in front of a truck on
the highway. But the walk down the mountain seemed too scary in the
dark.

from journal January 2013

showed up at her office every morning - calm, caring, and able to contain my horror. **She didn't seem disgusted!**

Part of an exercise Dahlia gave me was to encourage my younger self. I decided to be honest instead…

...I never showed her.

Letter to myself as a little girl
Welcome to the world little girl, this is it, this is your life. He's your dad,
God trusted you to him, so he has the right to do whatever he wants
with you.
Whatever comes your way was intended for you, so don't complain, don't
cry and don't think you can change it.
Do what you have to do, keep it to yourself. Don't tell anyone what a
bad kid you are, that's not gonna help.
So buff up and learn to take it cos it's gonna happen over and over and
over again.

Letter to myself as an older girl.
Girl, you can live through this, you just have to try harder. You can stop
whining coz things are not gonna get better. Just pretend, pretend that
you are someone else.
Some day you'll be big enough to make him stop or maybe ugly enough
for him not to want you.
You gotta be more careful, you gotta be better, of course this is gonna
happen when you mess up all the time. You gotta do better, be better
like your brother, be smarter.

Sarah Hemli

I gotta find a way to undo this. What was I thinking? I have to tell Dahlia that I made it all up, would she believe that? I did it for attention, I want Aaron's attention. It's my mind making up explanations for so many weird responses I have. Why am I so scared of people? Why do I always assume that they want to hurt me - make me do something I don't want to do?!

Maybe it just happened with my Grandpa - all the stuff with my dad I made up. Just one time with a man who has been dead for years. I must have made it all up with my dad, he wouldn't do something like that, he just wouldn't.

I was bad. He had to, he didn't want to, he had to, it was his job to teach me to be a good girl. God himself trusted him to do that job, I just made it really difficult.

I was not suppose to tell, never tell. Nobody will ever believe you. Why did I let this out, what was I thinking?!

It just didn't happen, it didn't, I would have remembered something all along, there would be something there. Those memories are just inhumane, nobody would do that to a little girl.

She must have asked for it, she must have wanted it, she kept messing up. He had to do it, she made him.

from journal January 2013

Dahlia gave me an other exercise to draw a picture of how I would **imagine** the future of my **wildest dreams.**

That's when a small **seed of hope** was planted. Could I survive facing reality? Could I learn to live with acknowledging the truth of my past? **Could anything good come from this?**

Sort through it all and stack it.
Use the rubble stacks to get out.
Crawl out of the hole with just a few pieces of rubble in my backpack,
whatever will be useful for the future.
Up. Out.
To the open horizon.

Sarah Hemli

In my wildest dreams

TIGHTrope
walking

I had **hope** when I left North Carolina. Dahlia, Mom Grace, and Papa Aaron. I felt cared for, loved, and believed in. **They all believed that I could get through this, so I did, too.**

Then I came home.

Bruce didn't understand my struggles. He tried to pressure me to open up to him. I did not have the capacity to let him in.

My relationship to my parents was shattered — only they didn't know that. They had been planning on visiting, which they did at least once a year.

It was all too much for me. **I was drowning.**

I kept coming back to the same conclusion — it would be better to end my life. **Better die than accept the reality of my past.**

Memories kept rolling in. When I least expected it, "movies" of my childhood played in my head. I called them "movies," because calling the memories would have been **acceptance of reality.**

Dahlia had me call every day to let her know I was OK. I hated making the phone calls. I didn't want her to hear my voice. Sometimes I had to follow up my phone message with an email of honesty. Eventually she agreed for me just to email her. That was easier.

I was so **overwhelmed by memories** and pain that I had no compassion for the little girl. I became angry with her. **She didn't fight**. She didn't say "no." Often times my dad barely had to say anything; she just did what he wanted. It made me furious. What was wrong with her? Why didn't she fight? **Why didn't she tell?**

I wanted her dead! I wanted me dead.

Living was too hard.

...My dad called today, he left a message, I plugged my ears as he was recording his message. I have to write that email .

It's not the first message he has left on the machine lately, it made Bruce think, he told me: "I know you won't tell me who it is, just tell me that it's not your dad". I didn't really respond, I was getting dinner ready for the kids. After dinner I went to Iris's house, I didn't want to risk any more conversation with Bruce tonight. I needed to buy some time to think. I don't know what to do.

part of email to Dahlia January 2013

Sarah Hemli

...Ok, so I'm not ok and I've been feeling bad for telling you that I am ever since I left the message. I'm sorry. Man, why is it so difficult for me to not tell you the truth?! I didn't use to have this problem.

Yesterday when Mila was at school and Matilda was sleeping, my mind went back to my plan from the other day, it just kept circling the possibility. I went upstairs away from the kitchen where the knifes are. It was this very un-emotinal weighing fore and against - benefits and disadvantages. I wrote in my journal for a while. As I was writing a new memory came - no, a new movie. It was a movie, it didn't happen, it couldn't have. But it's still really disturbing. Why is my mind doing this?!

Anyways, I went to Iris's house last night, they have a bible-study on Thursday nights, so I didn't talk to her much, but I was there.

Today I'm struggling with the movie from yesterday, I feel like I'm losing my mind. Not planning anything, though.

That's the truth, I'm sorry.

part of email to Dahlia February 2013

Oh, I've been debating what to tell you this morning - so long that it's not even morning anymore.

I'm ok - like I'm not gonna do something stupid, but my mind is really dark. I had another memory come up yesterday - somewhat similar to the one I told you about Monday. It's like I don't care anymore. If that really happened - nothing matters. My life is not even worth ending.

Bruce has decided that we are not gonna have sex for a long time - don't know why - so the one thing I have to give, he doesn't want. I'm useless to him - good for nothing.

I know you are gonna say that those feelings are probably connected to how I felt back then. It makes sense, but it's become who I am. It's what I work so hard to hide from people, I know they would run if they knew that I'm good for nothing but one thing.

It's ok if you don't want to talk to me anymore, I understand. It doesn't matter, I'm ok.

part of email to Dahlia February 2013

I'm not ok, I don't want to live, but I'm not gonna do anything about it. It just has too many consequences for you and other people, I can't do it - wouldn't be fair. I wish I had had the guts to do it at 13, it seems too late now - it would impact too many things. I wish it wouldn't.

part of email to Dahlia February 2013

Sarah Hemli

I never attempted anything aside from choosing **my best knife.** I held and touched it from time to time. I planned. I thought things through. I wondered if I could do it. **I wondered if heaven would be an option if I killed myself?!**

It gave me a sense of control. If I wanted, I could end it all and nobody could stop me.

In **moments of clarity**, I could admit to myself that I wasn't safe. They were short moments, but I did manage to call out for help.

Most of the time I numbed the pain with food, vine, television, or anything else that could drown out the pain and horror.

In the middle of my **helplessness**, I'd have a day here and there as **super women.** I'd be emotionally shut down, but have energy to get external things done. I would clean, cook, bake, sew, build, and be social. Like a machine, I would get so much done.

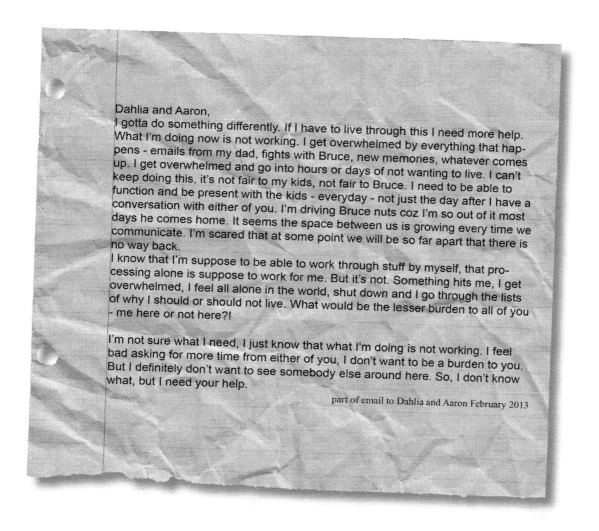

Dahlia and Aaron,
I gotta do something differently. If I have to live through this I need more help. What I'm doing now is not working. I get overwhelmed by everything that happens - emails from my dad, fights with Bruce, new memories, whatever comes up. I get overwhelmed and go into hours or days of not wanting to live. I can't keep doing this, it's not fair to my kids, not fair to Bruce. I need to be able to function and be present with the kids - everyday - not just the day after I have a conversation with either of you. I'm driving Bruce nuts coz I'm so out of it most days he comes home. It seems the space between us is growing every time we communicate. I'm scared that at some point we will be so far apart that there is no way back.
I know that I'm suppose to be able to work through stuff by myself, that processing alone is suppose to work for me. But it's not. Something hits me, I get overwhelmed, I feel all alone in the world, shut down and I go through the lists of why I should or should not live. What would be the lesser burden to all of you - me here or not here?!

I'm not sure what I need, I just know that what I'm doing is not working. I feel bad asking for more time from either of you, I don't want to be a burden to you. But I definitely don't want to see somebody else around here. So, I don't know what, but I need your help.

part of email to Dahlia and Aaron February 2013

I'm ok. I think my superwoman powers are wearing off. I still had them this early morning when I finally went to coffee with my 2 friends. They were just bursting to ask what I was doing when I was gone for a week. I told them a very little bit, I feel ok about it - even now.

I feel very distant from it all, numb. As I was talking to my friends about going to North Carolina to see this therapist, I almost felt like I was talking about someone else, not actually me. Maybe going back to the land of denial is a possibility.

part of email to Dahlia February 2013

I'm ok. New memory this morning, I want it to stop!

email to Dahlia March 2013

Sarah Hemli

I was **walking a tightrope**, balancing honesty with Dahlia with concealment of my darkest moments so she wouldn't call authorities and have me committed. I was less concerned about me,

then **my kids.** Grayson and Matilda were still foster kids. They'd be ripped out of our home and placed with a different family. My first adopted daughter, Mila, was removed repeatedly from a previous foster families, with lasting effects. **I couldn't let that happen** to my other two kids.

This fact kept me from doing anything rash, but some days my **desperation** was so strong that I nearly convinced myself that **everyone would be so much better off if I was not around.**

Dahlia was on to me.

Since she was far away, I agreed to see a local therapist. I didn't agreed so much as capitulate so she wouldn't make the call. I didn't like it, but she was right to give me the ultimatum. **I was not safe**.

I hated having to see Dr. K. One more person in the world would know what horrible things I'd done!

I downplayed it to Dahlia and to Dr. K.

Not living was so tempting. I didn't want to die. I just wanted not to live. They'd take my control away if I was honest with them.

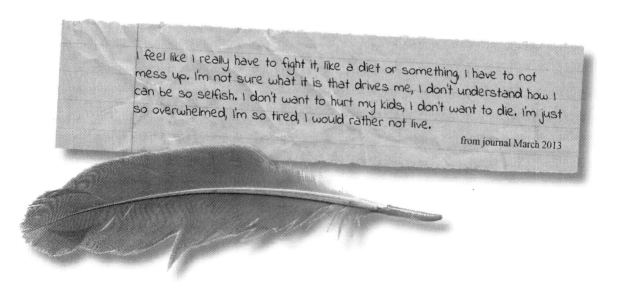

I feel like I really have to fight it, like a diet or something, I have to not mess up. I'm not sure what it is that drives me, I don't understand how I can be so selfish. I don't want to hurt my kids, I don't want to die. I'm just so overwhelmed, I'm so tired, I would rather not live.

from journal March 2013

A wake up call came when Bruce checked the Internet search history on my computer browser, and found that I had looked up "**how to commit suicide**". He freaked, so he called Aaron. I had to tell Dahlia and, for a full day, I did not know if she'd have me committed. The **agony** I went through thinking of what would happen to my kids was terrifying.

Dahlia,

I just got off the phone with Aaron and promised that I would email you. I'm ok now, I wasn't really earlier today. I went to bible study tonight at Iris's house and to the grocery store after. When I came home Bruce was on the phone with Aaron. We didn't have an appointment with him so it seemed kind of odd to me.

I didn't know what to tell you today, I went to my computer several times to email you. I was scared to tell you the truth coz I don't want you to react to it. I was scared not to. I wanted to climb in a hole somewhere and hide and not communicate with anyone. I wanted a break from me.

I woke up at 3 this morning and just had this sense that there's no way out of this. Today was hard, it was one of those days where time stands still. I just sat there and stared into the air wondering how I would make it through the day. My mind was so dark and I was fighting off the tears constantly. I tried to do something active, like you said, so I picked up the playroom in the basement, sorted and put toys in storage and cleaned the floors. It didn't make much of a difference, I was still there.

So tonight, I really didn't want to go anywhere, but Bruce wanted me to go, so I did and it was ok. On the way home I just felt numb and I was kind of relieved - numb is better than not wanting to go on.
But while I was gone Bruce looked up browser history on my computer and found that I had looked up "how to commit suicide" - he got scared and called Aaron.

Really, I'm not gonna do anything, I'm not planning anything. I just want to go to bed and try to have a better day tomorrow. I'm planning for tomorrow - we are having 2 families over for pizza night - 12 kids total. I plan to be around, today was just a really rough day for some reason.
I'm sorry.

email to Dahlia March 2013

Sarah Hemli

I fell back to the thought that **maybe it didn't really happen**. Being mentally sick seemed like a much better option. The only problem with that theory was that Dahlia didn't think anything was wrong with me, and Dr. K agreed that no mental diagnosis was evident. So I'd just claim that I had something neither of them had heard of.

It was my **escape**, my "**not really door**". - I've got to be crazy. It's gotta be made up. It couldn't have happened.

I'd **rather be crazy than have been abused**.

I'm ok - if I'm alone. I'm angry with me, disgusted by me, sad. I wish everyone would just leave me alone - stop needing me so much.

email to Dahlia March 2013

the NOT REALLY door

I had postponed **my parents visit** for a long time, but I'd have to let them come eventually. Really, I couldn't tell my dad no. I never could.

I knew I had to tell him something. Our relationship had to be redefined, but I didn't know how to talk to him. He knew I hadn't remembered my childhood. I had even expressed to him frustration of not remembering. Now, I wanted him to know that I knew.

And I wanted to see my mom. She was suffering from dementia and getting worse, so I wanted to see her even more.

I finally decided to let them come for three weeks . **I'd pretend for three weeks**. I believed I could do that and be fine.

Bruce still didn't know much of anything about what I was remembering. That had to change now that **my dad would be visiting**, because I was concerned for my girls. But first, I was anxious of Bruce's reaction. I was losing part of my control by telling him.

...my biggest fear might be that my dad's responds eliminates the "not really"- door completely - somehow that feels like the best and worst case scenario. I think I wanna tell him again that I remember my childhood, that it's not as wonderful and safe as they have always told us that it was. I think I want to tell him that I want to live in the truth, I think that might speak to him - that living in the truth is where God is. I don't think I want to specifically tell him what I remember.. what's the point - he already knows what happened - maybe?! I miss my mom.

part of email to Dahlia March 2013

Anyways, last night Bruce and I were sitting down together and I just told him. I first told him how nervous I was about his reaction and that he might take over control and try to change the decisions that I've made. And then I just told him - "you need to know who, coz he'll be here in May". He was shocked, he cried (which he never does), he began talking about how it didn't make any sense to him, how hard it was for him to believe, but he quickly got over himself. He really surprised me. I told him that I needed his help to keep the girls safe, to keep me safe and that I needed him to not talk about it or confront my dad. I asked him to pretend for 3 weeks and if he thought he could do that and he said yes. I felt like he actually listened to me and supported me, it was quite unbelievable! I even gave him a hug after and my quills didn't all stand up!

part of email to Dahlia April 2013

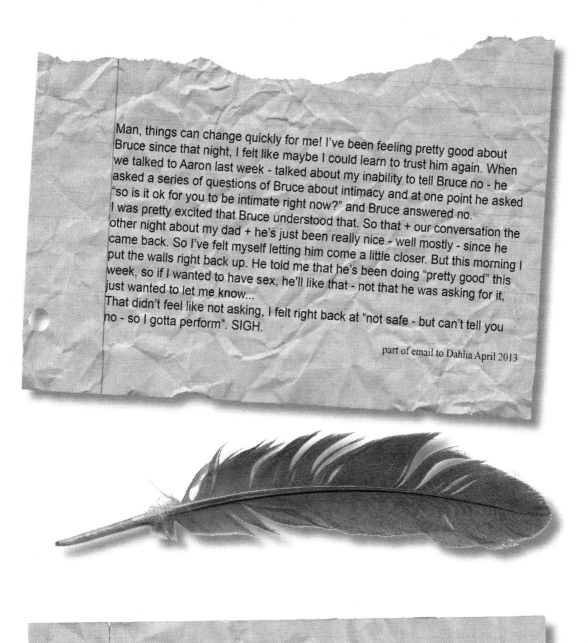

Man, things can change quickly for me! I've been feeling pretty good about Bruce since that night, I felt like maybe I could learn to trust him again. When we talked to Aaron last week - talked about my inability to tell Bruce no - he asked a series of questions of Bruce about intimacy and at one point he asked "so is it ok for you to be intimate right now?" and Bruce answered no. I was pretty excited that Bruce understood that. So that + our conversation the other night about my dad + he's just been really nice - well mostly - since he came back. So I've felt myself letting him come a little closer. But this morning I put the walls right back up. He told me that he's been doing "pretty good" this week, so if I wanted to have sex, he'll like that - not that he was asking for it, just wanted to let me know...

That didn't feel like not asking, I felt right back at "not safe - but can't tell you no - so I gotta perform". SIGH.

part of email to Dahlia April 2013

I'm completely overwhelmed. I just got my dad's itineraries. What have I done?

email to Dahlia April 2013

Thinking I got caught up in this whole story, that explains so many things I've always wondered about. It just can't be my story. It can't be his. I must be wrong.
Sarah

part of email to Dahlia April 2013

My dad called today, I picked up without checking caller id. The second I heard his voice I knew none of this happened, I made it all up. I don't know what to think now. I feel so confused and he is not even here yet.
Sarah

email to Dahlia April 2013

Sarah Hemli

Taste of
Freedom

So Super Woman is back in business - my house is clean, my kids are clean, 12 posts are cemented into the ground for the new barn, homemade bread, cake and pizza and more. It feels good to have all that stuff done, but I feel disconnected.

I've been ok with my dad today, I just don't like to look at him or be too close to him physically. He helped on the posts for the coop today and it was ok. I almost forgot.

What's gonna happen when Super Woman gets tired, though?!

part of email to Dahlia May 2013

Still just fine - just nothing. Well except for a sudden break down this morning. Bruce and I even had a big fight tonight, he was yelling at me. I didn't move, didn't cry, didn't feel anything.

part of email to Dahlia May 2013

My plan to **pretend** all was fine while my dad was here - **was a FLOP.** I went from numb to panic in seconds, but there was no "fine". Panic attacks. Memories. My body reacted with fear or freeze being close to him. I hadn't expected that. I was out of control, and I could not stop it.

My **hypervigilance was exhausting**. I constantly watched my little girls. If one of them were out of view for a minute, my mind flooded with images of what he could be doing to her, and I'd go find her.

My dad would pick up my girls and play with them. Whenever he put them on his lap to play horsey, I'd get **physically sick**.

My summer project was building a barn. I kept both my dad and I busy working on the barn. It helped distract my mind, and it kept us from having time to sit down and have to talk. My "not-really door" shriveled. It was three long, hard weeks.

Sarah Hemli

This afternoon+evening went all wrong. The kids got to me with their "I want this and I want that, why can't I have everything I want right here and now, you must not care about me"... and on and on.
I got totally overwhelmed with the demands, trying to meet their needs -but never good enough. I completely broke down while making dinner. I'm not even sure what really pushed the trigger, I just cried and cried with 4 spectators in shock. When Bruce came home at 6, dinner was still not done, but I was working on it crying.
Bruce got angry with the kids coz he thought they did something wrong and the kids began acting up coz they were scared about what was going on with me. So then I had even more that was my fault and more to cry about.
After getting soaked cleaning up building materials in the rain, I had come down some. But after dinner when Bruce left all leftover food and dishes on the counter and went upstairs, I broke down again. I tried to clean up, but realized that I needed to leave the kitchen and my chosen knife. I came back to it, looked at it for a while.
I asked Bruce to take the knives away and I've been in my bedroom since with a couple of glasses of wine, I think I can sleep.
I didn't want to do anything, really I didn't! I just want a break, I want it all to stop for just a little bit so I can catch my breath.

part of email to Dahlia June 2013

It almost felt as if things had been waiting for me to be less busy. The night after the wedding was misery, I couldn't really sleep, images/memories kept coming to me, very disturbing stuff that I couldn't really make sense of - YUCK!
When morning finally came Sunday - Bruce suggested we do something fun like a small road trip with the kids, so we spent all day driving and stopping at the beach, playgrounds, beautiful places = a lot of time not DOING anything. So things just continued in my head, a lot of it didn't make sense and I had no way to numb, no way to write or get by myself. It wasn't until we got home and kids were in bed, I could go outside to work and get a bit of a break from it all.
It doesn't make sense, my mind must be going crazy! Otherwise.. I'm ok.

part of email to Dahlia June 2013

It's hard to live in a constant state of anxiety — in **overwhelmed land**. I just wanted to cover it all up, put it away, zip it — as easy as stitching up a **deep, infected wound**. As I came to some kind of reluctant acceptance, memories kept coming.

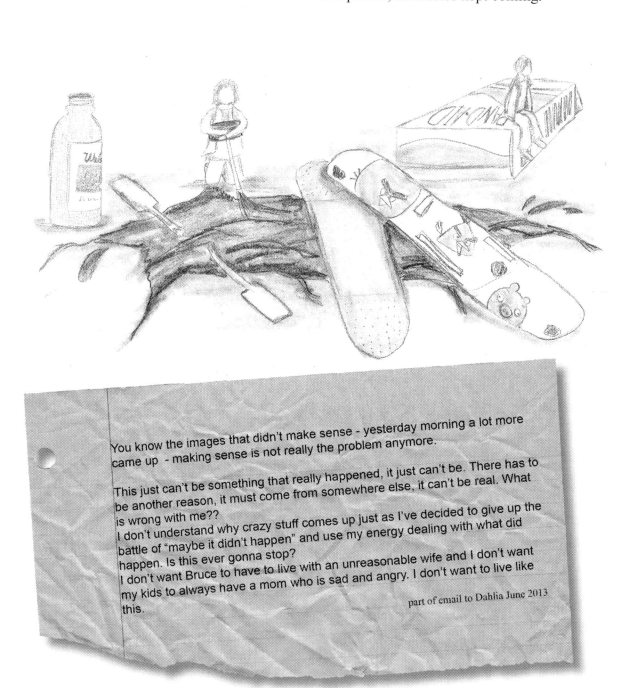

You know the images that didn't make sense - yesterday morning a lot more came up - making sense is not really the problem anymore.

This just can't be something that really happened, it just can't be. There has to be another reason, it must come from somewhere else, it can't be real. What is wrong with me??
I don't understand why crazy stuff comes up just as I've decided to give up the battle of "maybe it didn't happen" and use my energy dealing with what did happen. Is this ever gonna stop?
I don't want Bruce to have to live with an unreasonable wife and I don't want my kids to always have a mom who is sad and angry. I don't want to live like this.

part of email to Dahlia June 2013

Sarah Hemli

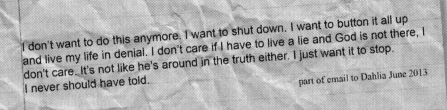

I don't want to do this anymore. I want to shut down. I want to button it all up and live my life in denial. I don't care if I have to live a lie and God is not there, I don't care. It's not like he's around in the truth either. I just want it to stop. I never should have told.

part of email to Dahlia June 2013

I want my "not really door" back. I want the doubt, the wondering, the internal war of "maybe it happened - maybe it didn't", I want the possibility of a mental disorder! How did I loose all that from one day to the next?! I don't want to face reality, I don't want to be the little girl under the table terrified coz she betrayed her dad. I don't want to be that!
Today has been big tear day. Every time one of the kids disobeyed - I cried. Matilda pulled a bunch of flowers out of a pot - I cried. She knocked her head in my face and hurt my lib - I cried. Mila was flailing on the couch next to me and pulled up my shirt - I cried.
I feel so out of control.

part of email to Dahlia June 2013

Memories that began emerging at this point were too much to carry. It was **overpowering**.

Although the first memories of my dad's actions were horrific, there was a sense of normalcy about them. I grew up with it. As much as I hated what he did, abuse by my dad was just part of my life.

The new memories had a whole **new level of terror, pain and fear** to them. My dad had given me away to other men. It all had happened at church.

I told myself, surely, these movies were **figments of my imagination.** The problem was that they were so clear. I remembered hearing the men sing a particular song in the sanctuary. I remembered what I was thinking at the time. I remembered words they spoke to me. **My body remembered.** I remembered **fighting for my life.** I remembered thinking the man was going to kill me. I remembered **giving up**.

I remembered the feelings of guilt and shame for betraying my dad and the special relationship only he and I had.

Just too much to carry!

After some time, I agreed to see Dahlia again. Nothing could be worse than how I'd been living. I was overwhelmed by what we worked out.

Aaron and Grace invited me to their home, and Dahlia had offered to come to Texas to meet me there. Mostly I was overwhelmed by my own choice, **I'd throw myself into the grueling work of revisiting my past.**

I believed Aaron and Grace cared about me. I felt special to Dahlia. Maybe I wasn't just another client to her. She'd have other things to do in Texas, but still, what therapist does that?

We were going to do Eye Movement Desensitization and Reprocessing (EMDR) therapy. I had researched it quite a bit. It seemed interesting in an intense, and scary way.

The first day meeting with Dahlia was not as bad as the first day in North Carolina, but it was still pretty bad. Speaking out the memories was a battle. I knew it was the path to get better, but **shame was dense**. I'd survived it already — I was just talking about it. It had already happened. But the emotions derived from reviewing my horror were intense. It was a good and horrific week.

I hated EMDR! Many details of the memories came up. My body remembered many things. There was no denying it. It happened. I hated it, because **EMDR worked!**

At the same time, I was with **my new family.** Aaron and Grace made me feel like a daughter to them. Their love and acceptance was **amazing**. Their daughter became like a sister to me — a sister full of joy and beauty. Just being around them was the most fun, peaceful, and healing experience.

I made progress that week. **Memories settled down**. It all felt more real, but more in the past. Toward the end of the week, we went to the lake. I took a long walk by myself along the shore. **I was at peace**. I knew what happened. I accepted it. The little girl, who I used to be, now had a voice. Her story was out. **She was free.** I could go on knowing it was **part of my past, no longer part of my present.**

Another week with Dahlia has flown by. I feel panicky. I'm scared to go home, scared to be alone.
This all happened, I'm not crazy I remember, my body remembers.

from journal August 2013

Sarah Hemli

I had a really nice time by the water yesterday. I went for a long walk by myself and I had this sense of peace about everything. The memories seemed more real but more in the past.

It felt like it was all part of me and although really sad, I was ok with it.

On the drive home new memories began coming back, oh man. I had hoped I was done.

This morning it continued until I got up and began interacting with the family.

Tonight we had a conversation with Bruce, I guess we will talk to you about it tomorrow - it ended with me crying in the bathroom and Aaron talking to Bruce by himself.

SIGH

email to Dahlia August 2013

For some reason, my **body issues** came up. I just got it. I didn't want to be fat anymore. I had no reason to. I felt in control, that I could keep myself safe. My words mattered, so I could say no and the world would have to listen.

I had always struggled with my weight. I'd **always thought I was fat**, even at times when I was not. Because of my stubborn nature, I was quite good at dieting, and I'd lose the same hundred pounds several times.

I used to blame my mother for my weight. As a child, I was always on a **diet**. My mom weighed me every Saturday. I knew I was too big. I weighed in at 35 kilograms (77 pounds), and I thought I was huge. I now look at the photo album and realize I really wasn't that big, but my mom feared I'd become fat. I had blamed my mom for setting me up to be overweight, telling me over and over again I'd always have to fight the scale. I thought she'd spoken some curse over me, and I had to pray my way out.

I now understood that the **fat was for my protection**. My words hadn't mattered then. I didn't have a voice with my dad or the other men. Nobody listened when I said no. Me objecting meant more anger and more pain.

But there was one way to create a **buffer between me and those men — fat**. It was hard to get fat when my mom controlled my diet, but as I became more independent, my body grew. I ate in secret. I stole chocolate from her freezer. I knew all her candy hiding places.

The pattern magnified in my adult life, when my mom wasn't around to limit my food intake. I didn't care about my body. I was **disgusted** by it. I hated my body for being fat. Really, my body was **fat because I hated it**. I blamed it for all those years when it was abused over and over again. It was just an object. I always **wished I could separate from it**.

As an adult, I would get to a point where I'd finally do something to get rid of this disgusting weight. I would go on a diet of deprivation and starvation and **lose 50, 70, 100 pounds**. Then I'd get into a relationship with a man and gain it all back. To get close to a man in **a small, attractive body was not safe.**

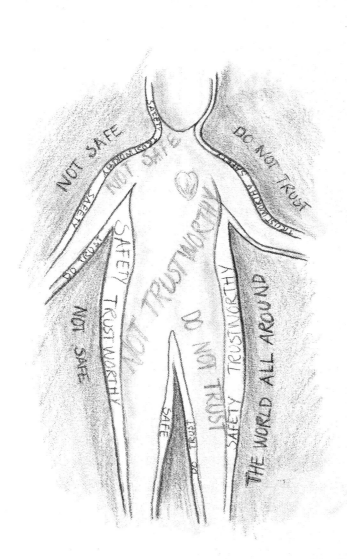

I was skinny when I met Bruce, beautiful, in fact, although I didn't know it at the time.

I finally understood. I **didn't need my fat anymore**. I could set other boundaries to keep myself safe. I hoped I could learn to care about me, learn to believe that **I was worth it**.

After my week in Texas, **life was different**. Well, for the most part. Some days were difficult. My relationship with Bruce was hard. I had become very different — **I mattered!** It was no longer all about him and what he wanted. I'd have a not-gonna-happen feeling whenever he would tell me how things were going to be or manipulate me. Parenting had become difficult, especially of my stepson, Nolan.

My dad finally responded to me telling him I remembered my childhood. He was vague, saying he'd probably done some dumb things when he was younger, but his heavenly father had forgiven him and he no longer remembered.

In all of it, there was hope and a strange sense of peace — **a fragile peace** — even in conflict.

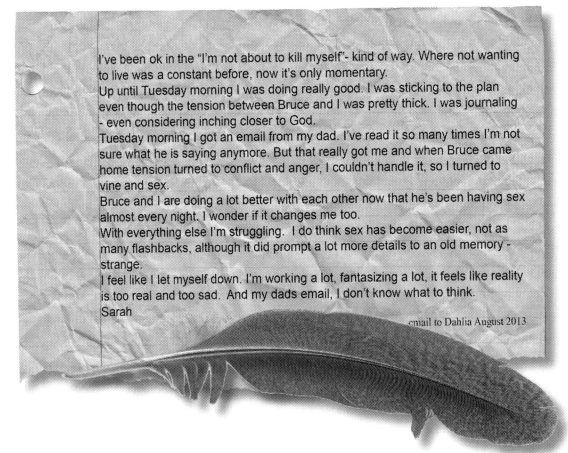

I've been ok in the "I'm not about to kill myself"- kind of way. Where not wanting to live was a constant before, now it's only momentary.
Up until Tuesday morning I was doing really good. I was sticking to the plan even though the tension between Bruce and I was pretty thick. I was journaling - even considering inching closer to God.
Tuesday morning I got an email from my dad. I've read it so many times I'm not sure what he is saying anymore. But that really got me and when Bruce came home tension turned to conflict and anger, I couldn't handle it, so I turned to vine and sex.
Bruce and I are doing a lot better with each other now that he's been having sex almost every night. I wonder if it changes me too.
With everything else I'm struggling. I do think sex has become easier, not as many flashbacks, although it did prompt a lot more details to an old memory - strange.
I feel like I let myself down. I'm working a lot, fantasizing a lot, it feels like reality is too real and too sad. And my dads email, I don't know what to think.
Sarah

email to Dahlia August 2013

I went into a fit of rage tonight... ...I was so angry with Nolan.
Later I realized he is acting just like Bruce, blaming me, the kids, whining, not
wanting to take responsibility. So am I taking it out on Nolan coz I know I can't
yell like that at Bruce?
Or where does that kind of rage come from?
And then I went downstairs and emptied the content of a fire extinguisher onto
myself and my laundry room, the valve just popped off. Lovely layer of white
dust everywhere!
I am tired.
Sarah

email to Dahlia August 2013

I've managed to control the rage today at least toward the kids, but its right under
the surface.

part of email to Dahlia September 2013

Dahlia, I took a bath tonight - like with water in the tub, just sitting there for
probably 15 minutes! Just coz I felt like it. I can't believe I was able to enjoy
that!
Bruce has been moping ALL day. He began the day at 6.30 storming into my
room yelling at me for Matilda being awake and waking everybody else up. Oh
dear, if I had the magic to make that child sleep past 5.30 I would so use it.
I think I did a pretty good job at shaking off the blame in the beginning of the
day - particularly when it would be for something I have no control over. It's
just so tiring.
The moping and the "I'm so sad about our sex life." drives me nuts. Tonight he
wouldn't even talk to me. But I took a bath !
Sarah

email to Dahlia September 2013

I had a new memory this morning. I was trying to get some more sleep while Matilda was playing in her room and everyone else was still sleeping. It just came, no trigger, nothing, just like that. I don't know what I'm more upset about - the actual memory or remembering.

10 minutes after Bruce came into my room and gave a speech about how this is not working for him. How he resents me for not having sex with him. Every night he is hoping that I'll change my mind and when I say good night and leave, he is filled with resentment. He's sick of talking to Aaron and sick of not being able to touch etc. his own wife. So he wants to be with other women, well he doesn't really want to, but what else is there to do!?

Now he's laughing and playing with the kids in the hallway and I'm the one crying in my room.

Sarah

email to Dahlia September 2013

I don't understand what is going on with me. I feel like I've regressed to something I don't want to be. I don't care about me, don't care about getting healthy. I'm cranky and angry with the kids.

Just last week I saw a doctor, he almost doubled my thyroid medication, I went to the dentist, Iris almost had me convinced that my knees should not hurt constantly, I was gonna go see a specialist.

All that seems like just stupid ideas now, I don't care, I don't deserve care.

I don't understand what happened.

Sarah

email to Dahlia October 2013

Sarah Hemli

I feel like a mess and I have no clue why. There's been nothing with Bruce, he's almost acting as if he cares about me.

Yesterday I worked nonstop, I had this "nothing" feeling all day. At the end of the day I felt right on the edge of falling apart. But when Bruce kind of asked for sex, I didn't really answer, I just left it open, I didn't know what I wanted. Part of me felt like I wanted to be used. By the time he came upstairs I pretended to be asleep.

I don't understand. This morning I feel nothing again.

email to Dahlia October 2013

Most of the day I had this overwhelming anger. I began yelling at Nolan at 6 this morning and it just continued.

I felt like anger was just boiling over. I felt like a horrible mom. I went down my old path of "I'm an awful person, my kids would be better off without me" for a little bit.

The anger kind of wore off toward the end of the day.

I'm just really tired.

Sarah

email to Dahlia October 2013

I hate me, I don't want to live with me.

Why is it that it's so important that I live? I know people think they would be sad if I wasn't here, but they don't really know me. This world would be a better place without me. I shouldn't have existed.

Bruce could find a beautiful wife who could give him what he needs and the kids could get a loving and patient mom. They deserve that.

I hate me, why do I have to live? I don't get it. I've been here long enough, why can't I just get out? Why is that so bad?

email to Dahlia October 2013

Bruce asked me on a date last night. It went pretty well as in we didn't get in a fight. Bruce was pushy - he touched me, tried to hold me, kiss me, hold my hand. It's like everything is ok between us in his mind, why should he not be doing all those things? I had vine, my own glass first and then Bruce's. it felt really good. Made sex easier too.
This morning I don't really feel anything.

email to Dahlia October 2013

I'm ok. I know Bruce is gonna call you. He decided I wanted to kill myself last night so he took knives away and then left the house. I'm so tired of his control. He demanded to know if I had talked to you about it. Not his business I told him, so now he's gonna call you.
Can we talk?
Sarah

email to Dahlia October 2013

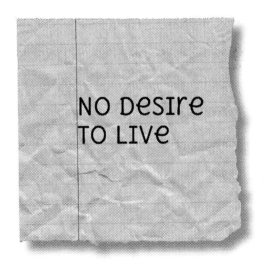

I did well for a couple of months. I was **able to sustain** the hope, the belief that I mattered, and my right to make my opinion known, but it wore off. **I became unstable**. Most days, I'd barely **function**. I got up and did what needed doing. I took care of my kids. But I was counting the minutes for the days to be over.

Other days, I'd have a **glimmer of hope**. I'd consider that maybe someday life would be worth living. Maybe there was a **purpose for my existence**. Maybe, just maybe.

I'd do OK for a while, and then new memories surfaced. I'd spend days waiting for life to be over.

Anger lurked under the surface at all times!

I was exhausted!

Sarah Hemli

Today has been so - I don't even know what to call it - I wish this life could just be over, I don't want to do this anymore. I didn't drink or have sex and I'm not gonna kill myself. I just wish it could be over.

email to Dahlia November 2013

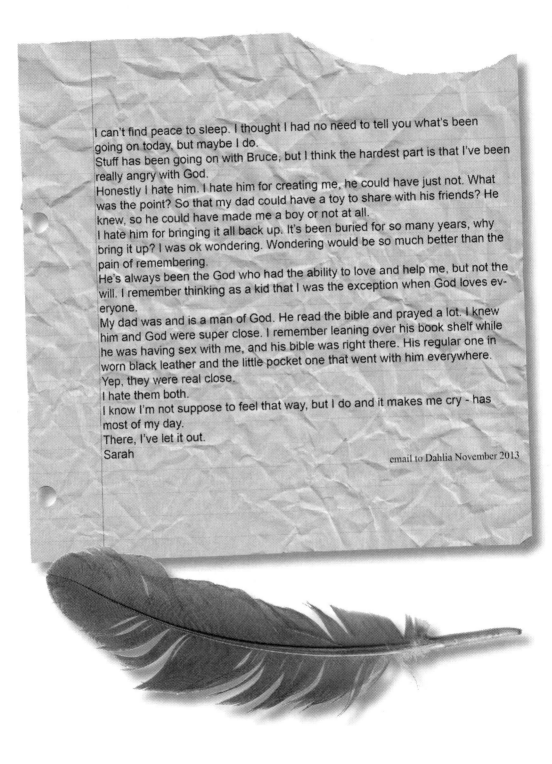

I can't find peace to sleep. I thought I had no need to tell you what's been going on today, but maybe I do.

Stuff has been going on with Bruce, but I think the hardest part is that I've been really angry with God.

Honestly I hate him. I hate him for creating me, he could have just not. What was the point? So that my dad could have a toy to share with his friends? He knew, so he could have made me a boy or not at all.

I hate him for bringing it all back up. It's been buried for so many years, why bring it up? I was ok wondering. Wondering would be so much better than the pain of remembering.

He's always been the God who had the ability to love and help me, but not the will. I remember thinking as a kid that I was the exception when God loves everyone.

My dad was and is a man of God. He read the bible and prayed a lot. I knew him and God were super close. I remember leaning over his book shelf while he was having sex with me, and his bible was right there. His regular one in worn black leather and the little pocket one that went with him everywhere.

Yep, they were real close.

I hate them both.

I know I'm not suppose to feel that way, but I do and it makes me cry - has most of my day.

There, I've let it out.

Sarah

email to Dahlia November 2013

Sarah Hemli

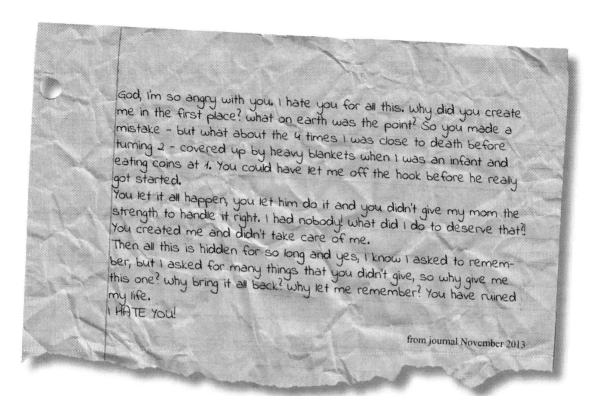

God, I'm so angry with you. I hate you for all this. Why did you create me in the first place? What on earth was the point? So you made a mistake - but what about the 4 times I was close to death before turning 2 - covered up by heavy blankets when I was an infant and eating coins at 1. You could have let me off the hook before he really got started.

You let it all happen; you let him do it and you didn't give my mom the strength to handle it right. I had nobody! What did I do to deserve that?! You created me and didn't take care of me.

Then all this is hidden for so long and yes, I know I asked to remember, but I asked for many things that you didn't give, so why give me this one? Why bring it all back? Why let me remember? You have ruined my life.

I HATE YOU!

from journal November 2013

I had **no desire to live**.

I had come to the conclusion that ending my life wasn't an option because of my kids. I was furious with God that he had let me live through the abuse of my childhood. I was angry He brought all this back now that I had kids to care for. I was **out-of-control angry!**

I struggled with my **relationship** with Bruce. He struggled with his own issues.

The mix was toxic.

My new found worth was sensitive, and Bruce's demands were great. He had a hard time realizing that I was my own person and I had an opinion about when and how and how often sex should happen.

I came into the marriage thinking my purpose in our relationship was to provide sex. It's what I had learned from childhood, but I didn't want that to be true for me anymore. I didn't want my marriage to be a repeat of my childhood, when I was an object to fulfill a man's desires. I **wanted more purpose in our marriage**.

We tried couples **counseling**. We saw the counselor for a while. It seemed useless — he was disrespectful and full of himself — but it gave me a place where I could practice being me. I chose to tell him my story and later also what I thought of him and that his approach was not helpful. It was **empowering**.

Last night when Bruce came home he walked in and kind of cornered me in the kitchen and put his arm around me. I wiggled out and he was clearly dis-appointed.
It made me think about how his physical advances make me feel. My body reacts as if he's gonna hurt it. So tonight I told him that I need a break from anything physical. Don't want him to ask for hugs or kisses, don't want him to just do it...

...I think I did pretty well in the conversation, I didn't take his problems for him. I guess in his mind I just added a big problem to him. I did ask him several times if he would be willing to respect this boundary, he never answered. We'll see.
Sarah

part of email to Dahlia November 2013

Dahlia, I did it. I told him. Dr. P that is, I told him my story. I also got to talk to him about other things - everything that I had written down. And then I just asked him if I could tell him, he said sure, so I did.
Oh goodness - one more person knows. I didn't think of it that way until just now.
Sarah

part of email to Dahlia November 2013

I don't really want to be a wife or a mother for that matter. What is the pur-pose of living except getting it over with? I don't mean it in a self-pity-suicidal kind of way, I just don't get it. Why am I here - what's the point?!
Still cry-e but ok. Gonna have a drink and watch a movie.
Sarah

part of email to Dahlia December 2013

Sarah Hemli

I don't understand why I do this, I hate being in this place, I feel so powerless here.

I feel like selfishness has swallowed me up, I don't care about anything or any body. I know the kids would be much better off without me, I know Bruce would be better off. I try to tell myself that's not true, but I just know.

I know I'm not suppose to think about dying, so I think about running away, disappearing. Leaving everyone behind, set them free from the burden of me. I just want to not be.

I know we've talked about this and that I'm not suppose to do this, I don't know how it happens. I don't know why.

I hate how I talk to the kids, I have no tolerance for them, I just want them to leave me alone. That's not who I wonna be, why can't I stop this?

email to Dahlia December 2013

I still struggle with glimpses of memories come up, it's just never a good time. Tonight as I was rocking and singing to Matilda - and then memories - what on earth?!

Last night I was up a lot with Grayson so I spent several hours in that not awake not asleep state. Not a good place for me to be, it's like free reign for memories. Sarah

email to Dahlia December 2013

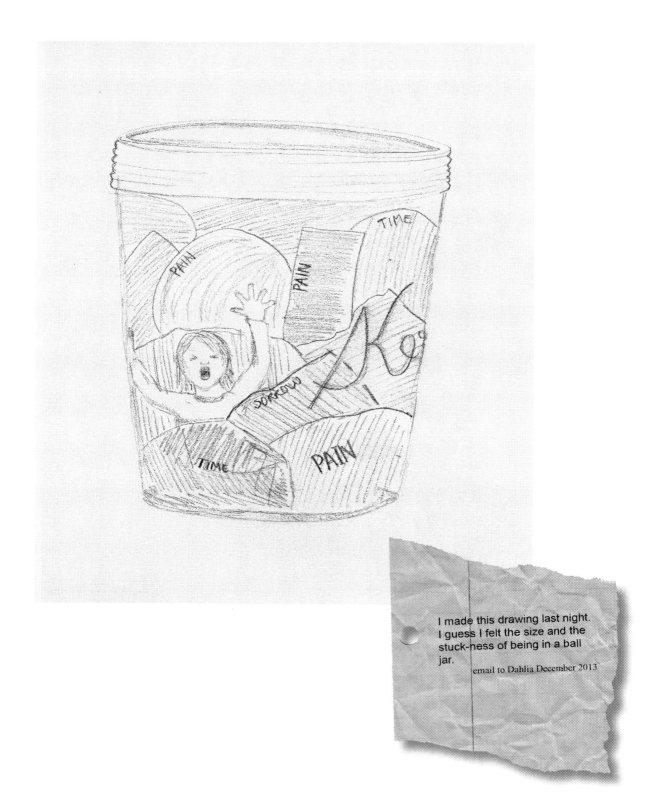

I made this drawing last night. I guess I felt the size and the stuck-ness of being in a ball jar.

email to Dahlia December 2013

Sarah Hemli

I had a strange experience this morning driving to school, it wasn't really a memory, but my body was reacting as if it was. I'll tell you about it tomorrow. It took a practical project when I got back home to kind of shake it.
Sarah

part of email to Dahlia December 2013

I'm gonna scream! I'm so sick of memories. I feel like this wrist memory is just lurking in the shadows for me to have an unattended moment.
After running around all day I had to go into town as soon as Bruce came home. So all alone in the car - peace - memory - my body reacting. I get stuck, I can't make it stop.
I want it to stop.
Sarah

part of email to Dahlia December 2013

I so want to heal. I want to move on, I want to use it all for good. I want to be whole, I want to be free.
As I'm healing my marriage is in shambles. I really don't know how things are gonna go from here. I'm exhausted, I feel invisible, not cared for. I wonder if it's ever gonna change. I dream of a better life, of happiness, wholeness, energy, love. But how do I get here?!

from journal December 2013

I hate me, I hate me so much. I hate every inch of my skin and every ounce of my body. I hate every thought in my mind and every word that comes out of my mouth. I hate that I don't have a choice. That you God decided that I should live. Did you ever stop to consider if that was a good plan?...

from journal December 2013

I drew these a few days ago - box and boulder scenarios. For the past almost-week I've lived with the wine bottle there too and I've been ok. Today I went back on my diet which does not include alcohol. It was really hard, but not so much missing the treats and food. I just like me better with alcohol, I'm much nicer, I can handle more - actually I think I become less introverted. Being around everybody all the time has not bothered me until today.
Today I've had times where I had to fight "out of the blue" - tears, Bruce's comments get to me, the kids drive me nuts. I feel like nobody listens to me or cares. And I'm not fun to be around, that's just not who I want to be.

part of email to Dahlia December 2013

Sarah Hemli

One of the tools Dahlia taught me was having a **mental box**. When memories came up, I put them in the box to take care of later. It helped my visual mind, but it was **hard to get stuff to stay in** there. I pictured myself sitting on the box to make sure nothing leaked out.

A boulder was also needed, and, at times, alcohol seemed necessary.

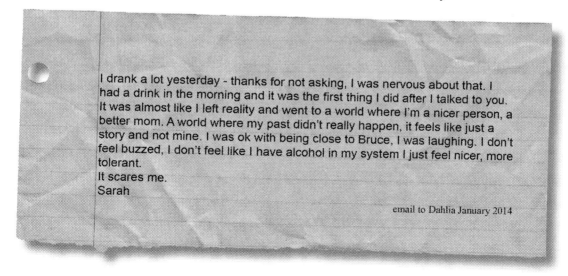

I drank a lot yesterday - thanks for not asking, I was nervous about that. I had a drink in the morning and it was the first thing I did after I talked to you. It was almost like I left reality and went to a world where I'm a nicer person, a better mom. A world where my past didn't really happen, it feels like just a story and not mine. I was ok with being close to Bruce, I was laughing. I don't feel buzzed, I don't feel like I have alcohol in my system I just feel nicer, more tolerant.
It scares me.
Sarah

email to Dahlia January 2014

in denial

Then followed the most **indecisive** and wavering time in this process. The "wrist" memory was bad. It began coming back to me as a body memory. I was trying to take of my coat while driving and my wrist got stuck in my sleeve. My whole body panicked. In the coming days bits and pieces of it emerged. I couldn't believe it. It was **too horrifying**. It didn't make sense. It overwhelmed me. There was something about it that made it **painful on a whole new level**. I was not going to accept this one without a fight!

I wanted to get through it all, but I struggled to stay in that place. I would still take some big **dips in the sea of hopelessness**.

I cycled through three different possibilities for the road ahead — three different ways for me to deal with the memories, the shame, the guilt, the pain — all the rubble that had come out when I opened the door to the hidden and forgotten unknown. Honestly, I knew there was only one option that would let me move ahead. The other two would just stall me. Eventually, I'd have to pick Door #1.

Stalling had its benefits: avoiding pain, avoiding responsibility, avoiding the growing realization of what happened to me and how it was affecting me every day of my life.

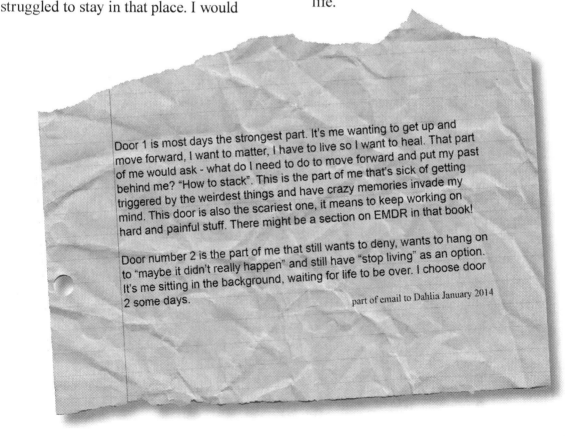

Door 1 is most days the strongest part. It's me wanting to get up and move forward, I want to matter, I have to live so I want to heal. That part of me would ask - what do I need to do to move forward and put my past behind me? "How to stack". This is the part of me that's sick of getting triggered by the weirdest things and have crazy memories invade my mind. This door is also the scariest one, it means to keep working on hard and painful stuff. There might be a section on EMDR in that book!

Door number 2 is the part of me that still wants to deny, wants to hang on to "maybe it didn't really happen" and still have "stop living" as an option. It's me sitting in the background, waiting for life to be over. I choose door 2 some days.

part of email to Dahlia January 2014

Sarah Hemli

Door number 3 is me wanting to move on, but nervous to. I crave to be cared for, I've never know care much until this past year, I always took care of myself. I have experienced a lot of care and support the past year, but I still crave it. Sometimes I wish I could do the week in North Carolina with Aaron and Grace and you over - as awful as it was, just to re-experience the level of care I was given. This is me scared that if I move forward and put my past behind me I might have to fend for myself alone again, that I would lose people who have walked with me through this. Some nights when I can't sleep I fantasize of being cared for somehow, I don't quite understand why this is so strong in me.

part of email to Dahlia January 2014

Sometimes I wonder if it's time to go back to pretend land to make my marriage work. Maybe I could still fake stuff, I have the skills I just have to find a way to pacify my heart.

But then I think about what it feels like to have value. To take the time and energy to keep healing. To allow myself to trust that some people actually care about me. To receive care and love without pushing people away. To take care of myself - lose weight, get help. To not numb! To pay attention to my needs - just to have it be ok for me to have needs, to have boundaries, to have "wants". Such a fragile view of myself, but it feels good.

from journal January 2014

Sarah Hemli

I thought about this after we talked, it seems really silly, I don't know if I can explain it. I still fear that if I tell someone they won't believe me. I think about it every time I share the littlest bit - how do I say this in a way that they will believe me? It seems so ingrained in me that nobody will believe me, I don't remember him ever telling me, I've just always known I guess.

Even with you - I consider what you think of what I say. I know, I should really know by now that you do believe me, I do know that. I just entertain the "what ifs" - what if we did EMDR and something came up that made you say - "oh, now I get it, never happened, you are just crazy."

part of email to Dahlia January 2014

Trauma-kid get together this morning. We lost power at 3am and both Mila and Grayson were freaking out = kept coming to my room to make sure that the house was not gonna burn down. Trauma logic I guess. (Funny how I've become a lot more tolerant of their non-rational fears) I dozed off in between "visits" and had parts of the memory show up.

After a couple of hours like that I went to YouTube on my phone to watch something different. And eventually daylight and power came back.

So 3 very tired people today. It's like I can't shake it off, it feels stuck in my body in particular.

Sarah

email to Dahlia January 2014

It's time to shut down, zip it up, put it away, leave it behind, never speak of it again. It's time to push people away - get back to safety where nobody knows, Its time to pretend, I did it before, I can do it again. I must be able to!

Why did I think things could get better? Why did I think telling would bring anything good?

I gotta stop talking to Dahlia, I shouldn't be trusting her like that, she is way too close, I should never have told her. I should have known better.

from journal January 2014

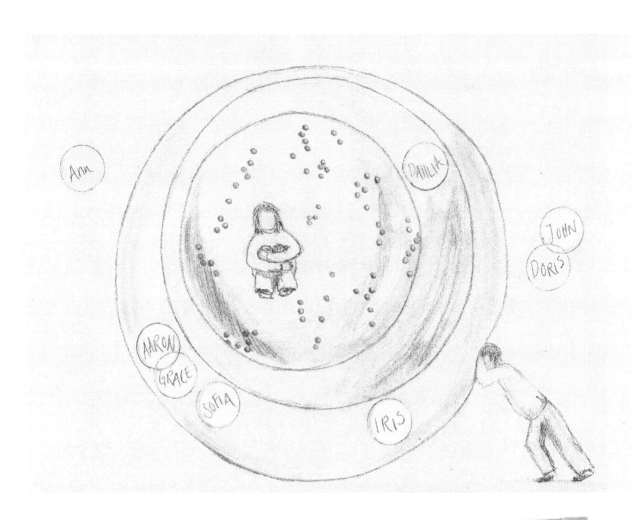

I drew something tonight - my sad/isolated feeling kind of grew as the day went by, so I wanted to do something with it = bubbles. 3 bubbles inside each other. I'm alone in the inner one with a bunch of little bubbles - I think they are memories I've never spoken. You are in the next bubble and Aaron, Grace, Sofia and Iris in the third one. Outside is Bruce trying to push his way in.

part of email to Dahlia January 2014

I hated our conversation today, I feel like I've given up. I felt like I was wasting your time. I don't understand what's happening with me, where's the person who was gonna get through this whatever it would take?
I don't want to ever talk about my past again.
I had a conversation with Bruce yesterday, he's encouraging me to go see you, he's willing to work things out. He said - "just give me about 2 weeks notice to clear things with work and find you airline tickets". -could he make it any easier for me? I know Iris will help out with Matilda.
Why am I not moving - I know letting it out would help, I know just telling you would make it easier to carry. I know how much better I felt after last week of EMDR. I feel paralyzed.
I think about doing EMDR again and I cringe. What a wimp!

email to Dahlia January 2014

Today I feel numb most of the time, really tired, crinkled up and heavy inside. I struggle with getting really angry over the littlest things the kids do, and Bruce is irritated because he can tell I'm struggling, but he doesn't get any details, so I'm rejecting him.
I did go see Iris for a little while this morning. It's difficult to hear how worried she is about me. She says that if she was in my shoes she would have gone under a long time ago. I don't think it's that bad.

email to Dahlia January 2014

We went to some friends for dinner tonight, I really didn't want to go - considered faking an instant sickness, but I ended up going.
During dinner this man that I had just met pulls out his fabric handkerchief. My stomach turned, my salad wanted to come back out, I had to concentrate on breathing for a few minutes. All for a stupid handkerchief just like my dads.
I don't know - is that that bad?
I IM-ed with my friend Sofia today. She's gonna be in Texas in March, she really wants me to come out and it might be possible for me to go. Both her and Aaron, Grace and Jolee are so excited that I might be able to be there. I'm not really. That's just kind of overwhelming to me.
So I don't know - is that that bad?
I guess I'm thinking that right now is bad but I'm gonna get it together again, just need a little time.
Am I in denial?

email to Dahlia January 2014

Dahlia responded "yes"

Sarah Hemli

I drew this tonight. I'm so confused by myself. One day I'm gonna get through this and the next day I'm just gonna sit and wait for life to be over. The past days I've been so numb, I even had sex with Bruce and felt nothing - well maybe shame the next day. Before that I was so overwhelmed and before that I was gonna do whatever it would take - before that who knows?!

I feel embarrassed and angry with myself - what do I get out of wavering instead of choosing what to do and keep with it?

email to Dahlia January 2014

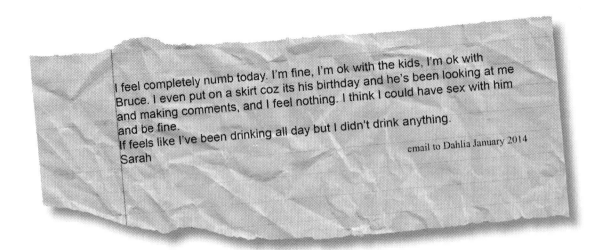

I feel completely numb today. I'm fine, I'm ok with the kids, I'm ok with Bruce. I even put on a skirt coz its his birthday and he's been looking at me and making comments, and I feel nothing. I think I could have sex with him and be fine.
If feels like I've been drinking all day but I didn't drink anything.
Sarah

email to Dahlia January 2014

Dahlia was right; **I was in denial**. I was in a bad place, and things were not just going to get better without me making better choices for myself.

The memories were **horrific and intrusive. There was no way around them**.

I was like a toddler throwing a tantrum, kicking and screaming; I knew what really happened, but I didn't want to remember. I didn't want to work through it. I wanted to deny it. I wanted to kick and scream and deny — anything to forget what I remembered.

All of that and daily life, with four special needs kids and a strained relationship with Bruce, was going to take me down,

if I didn't do something. **Yeah, not that bad, I'm just shutting down!**

At one point, I **almost gave up**. Actually, I did give up. I was too tired to make the decision to fight. Dahlia had told me that taking a break would be an option, so that's what I told her.

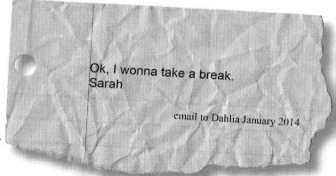

Ok, I wonna take a break.
Sarah

email to Dahlia January 2014

What I really meant was

"**I'm done!**"

The **voice** in my head that I listened to — after all this time working through stuff — was still much the same and so very **hard to escape**.

- "you are not worthy of health, you don't deserve to live without pain. You deserved what happened to you and now you gotta live with it. So get yourself together and get over it. It happened a long time ago and nobody cares now, you have to pay people to care. You didn't deserve all the help and care and attention you got already and you certainly don't deserve more. You are a burden, you are not worthy of help."

part of email to Dahlia January 2014

I can't figure out what I really need. Between my fears, my ability to numb and my considerations of other people, I just don't know.
I think I'm mostly numb these days, I'm trying to keep the latest memory away from my mind and its working somewhat. My stomach is a knot.
I still run into these little things of everyday life that makes my inside turn and time stand still.
I have very little tolerance for Bruce and the kids.
I have not been doing many breathing exercises but I think I have used some of the coping skills. I do take time for myself in the evening in spite of Bruce's sad puppy eyes. I've done more journaling and drawing.
I think I'm doing better than a couple of weeks ago or maybe I'm just number. I don't know.
Sarah

email to Dahlia January 2014

I didn't want to accept the validity of the memories from the church. In general, **I couldn't wrap my mind around** the fact that a man would take a seven- or eight-year-old girl to what looked like a men's prayer meeting and let other men be with her. But **that it was my dad was just unbelievable**.

The memories were vivid and filled with so much **pain** and **shame**. Going to see Dahlia for more EMDR treatment was agreeing to re-live those horrible moments. **Who would want to do that?**

I had weeks of **roller coaster rides**. One day, I'd be determined I was going to get through this and do the work I needed to. I'd go see Dahlia again, **do EMDR again and survive!** I'd come out on the other side and be okay. The next day, I'd feel utterly hopeless, **waiting for life to be over.** I wanted to die, and knowing that that was not an option made everything worse.

I was **exhausted, overwhelmed** by memories, if not just **numb**. Emotionally spent, I had to do something.

Dahlia offered for me to come see her again and I immediately said no! There was no way I was going to impose on her time like that again. **I should not need another intensive time** with her. Plus she would not let me come alone. I'd have to have someone there with me. I really didn't want to go, but then I did. I didn't want to ask Aaron and Grace to come with me, but then I wanted them there. I definitely didn't want to do EMDR again. I hated it, but then I wanted to give it my all so I could find **peace** again.

Sarah Hemli

Dahlia,
A couple weeks ago you talked about options for me, you said you had the "bandage" feeling again. So tell me this: Is there a way that I can move forward without seeing you in person or seeing somebody else here?
It's become very black and white to me - move forward = visit North Carolina or button things up, stop talking about it = stay here.
I talked to Aaron. It was good to talk to him, I'm not sure why I've been not wanting to talk to him. I told him about the conflict between wanting to hide and wanting to move on, and how when I felt that going to North Carolina wasn't an option then I wanted it.
You can probably guess how the conversation went after that!
He spent a long time trying to convince me that it wouldn't be an inconvenience to them, that they like being around me, that I'm not a burden etc.
I spent a long time saying no, no, no. That's too much to ask. (But really in the back of my mind I was going 'I'm not worth it')
Aaron replied -"you're not asking, but we can offer".
So Aaron is on it. They have some airline miles that he's gonna check on, coz really we don't have the money for 3 tickets. And then he asked me to email you - so VERY hypothetically I'm doing that.
When would work for you and how many days? Would you be willing to work over a weekend? Aaron and Grace have stuff happening in March and April, so Aaron's suggesting February - but that's really soon!
Sarah

email to Dahlia January 2014

Meltdown today -even though I spent the morning at Iris's house. Spent the past 3 hours in my office, drew this.
Wonna give up.
Sarah

email to Dahlia January 2014

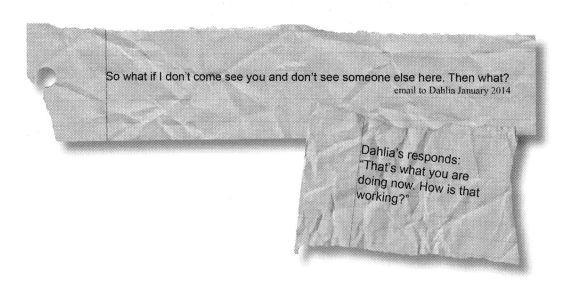

So what if I don't come see you and don't see someone else here. Then what?
email to Dahlia January 2014

Dahlia's responds: "That's what you are doing now. How is that working?"

Sarah Hemli

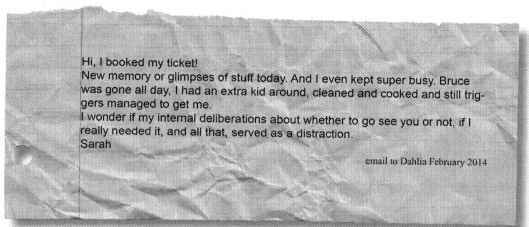

I spent months thinking about what to do. It wasn't until I actually **made a decision** and began planning to go that it dawned on me what I had been doing — **distraction**. It was easier to focus on the question of doing another intensive therapy or not, than to focus on the fact that I was overwhelmed and worn out, having new intrusive memories, and being triggered in my everyday life to a point of **not functioning.**

How do you live when you really don't want to?!

I had a hard time getting over myself when I thought about the people involved. How could I take Dahlia's time? How could I inconvenience Aaron and Grace to come out again? How do I receive that kind of attention when I know myself to be **worthless and without meaning?**

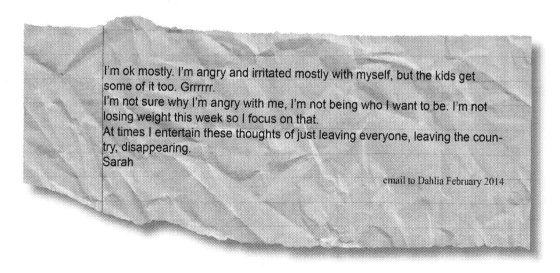

I drew this today. I feel like a monster, I get irritated and angry so easily. I yell and say dumb things.

I'm not sure why it's such a young girl inside the monster, I just meant it to be me, but a much younger Sarah felt like the right thing to put there. It just doesn't make sense to me.

email to Dahlia February 2014

Sarah Hemli

LETTING GO

Dear little girl,
what's up? what is it that you want to say? what is it that you need from me?
I see you in your little spencer, you were wearing that when you were 2, I remember seeing it in pictures. And I remember your baby doll dressed in the striped suit. I see you, what do you need?
Do you feel overlooked - forgotten? what your dad did at home almost seemed normal compared to what happened at the church. what happened at home was bad! Something in you died then when you were only 2 - innocence, confidence, trust, belief in the world and people around you, self worth.
Everything changed then. From then on you were a bad girl, you were only what you could do for others. Attention, love, care, time had to be earned. The world no longer a safe place to be and people could not be trusted.
Your existence went from living to surviving.
I understand that you are angry, little girl. You lost so much, it was taken from you. I don't know if I can ever give some of it back to you, but I can try.
You didn't even know how wrong it was in the beginning. I remember situations that seemed more like a game. But I think there was something in you that knew things were not right.
Sarah

February 2014, translated from danish

I couldn't believe I was doing this again. Once again, I was overwhelmed by the willingness, care, and love that was extended to me.

I had lived my life thinking I was only worthy of connection with other people if I gave them what they wanted. **What began with my dad had extended into all relationships**. My value was in doing, in performing, in what I could offer. So to have Dahlia be happy to spend another week with me, and Aaron and Grace come out to be with me, was **unbelievable**! That they didn't mind, that I didn't even have to ask.

I now know other people love me, but I had always made their love conditional. I hadn't understood unconditional love. It was ingrained in me to **fulfill other people's needs** in order to have **self-worth**.

I had fulfilled this in all my relationships with men. I had **erased myself** to fit whatever a man wanted from me. Growing up, I lived in constant hypervigilance to stay as safe as possible. My dad was an unsafe factor in my life, so being able to read him and see things coming added at least a sense of control to my life. I had a well-developed ability to watch and discern what a man wanted from me, and I was well trained to give him whatever that was.

I had **fulfilled this in my marriage**. It's who I was when I met Bruce. Without even noticing, I had **conformed** to what he wanted and needed. I thought I had a good marriage. Sure there were things that I'd like to be different, but for the most part it was okay — until I **began changing**.

What if I didn't have to be invisible?

What if I mattered?

What if it wasn't just Grace and Aaron and Dahlia that thought I mattered; that I was worth time, care, and effort just because of being me. What if I really did matter?!

There I was, back in North Carolina spending the first morning hanging out with Aaron and Grace. I had nothing to do, nothing to give. All I could do was **be** and drink coffee. More amazing was that I was good enough. I could be me, and that was good enough. I didn't have to constantly consider how others felt about my every move.

Then came the afternoon, when I was to meet with Dahlia.

Disbelief comes in waves.

It was hard for me to work with Dahlia, because I wanted for it all to be made-up. The **protective notion** that maybe it didn't really happen was loud the first day, although I knew my memories were real. I desperately wanted them not to be.

As I questioned again the validity of my memories, a war raged in me. **I had no peace**. I was wasting this blessing of face-to-face time with Dahlia.

After spending the first afternoon with Dahlia, I **wrote a letter** to my little-girl self. After I wrote the first couple of lines, **peace washed over me**. I

> Dear little girl,
> Listen up now, this is serious! For the last time I'm gonna ask you - did this really happen? You have to let me know now if you made it all up. It's ok if you did as long as you tell me the truth.
> I believe that you have told the truth. I believe you. I don't understand how anyone could hurt a little girl like that, but they did.
> I know that you made it through it all. you survived by pretending and not feeling. But we are not gonna live like that anymore. You can stop now, let your mind let go. I know you are trying to think about many other things - to think away from it all. But right now we are here and this week we are gonna think about it.
> You are a good girl if you tell the truth and let go of secrets. Now is the time to let go, this is serious!
> We can trust these people, they want what's good for us, they can help. Heath is on our side and I'm gonna take care of stuff. We have to live through it one more time to find peace. It's not gonna be forgotten, you are not gonna be forgotten. Just tell the truth and I'll take care of the rest.
> Sarah

February 2014, translated from danish

became calm. I knew the truth and I was able to contain it.

Everything in me was **resisting doing EMDR**. I couldn't do it. I knew what it felt like. I knew the pain of living through the situations again. I knew the **unpredictability** of what my mind would remember. I didn't want to do it. Some of the roughest memories I had not yet spoken about, they were still in hiding. There were parts that I didn't remember. I didn't want to remember more.

Doing EMDR was **letting go of control**. In just talking, I could decide which memories to keep hidden, which details to push away. I could distance myself. Doing EMDR was deliberately placing myself in the middle of the mess, not knowing where my mind would go next.

Again, I wrote to my little girl to make sense of what was about to happen. I had to try to get her to a place where the goal no longer was to remember to forget. To instead go through this painful process, let go of the memories, and come out on the other side.

Sarah Hemli

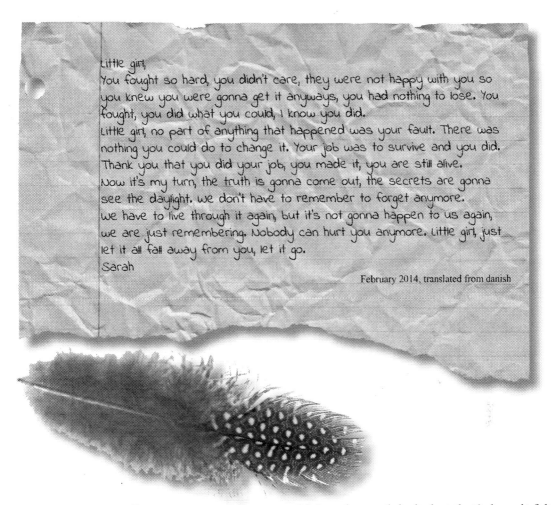

Little girl,
You fought so hard, you didn't care, they were not happy with you so you knew you were gonna get it anyways, you had nothing to lose. You fought, you did what you could, I know you did.
Little girl, no part of anything that happened was your fault. There was nothing you could do to change it. Your job was to survive and you did. Thank you that you did your job, you made it, you are still alive.
Now it's my turn, the truth is gonna come out, the secrets are gonna see the daylight. we don't have to remember to forget anymore.
we have to live through it again, but it's not gonna happen to us again, we are just remembering. Nobody can hurt you anymore. Little girl, just let it all fall away from you, let it go.
Sarah

February 2014, translated from danish

The next day, I was **reluctant**, but **calm**. I **hated every second of EMDR**. The emotions were strong, the memories awful to go through. Letting them out was a mix of **relief and fear** — relief that I no longer carried it all alone, and fear based in an old and deep belief that I should never tell!

For some reason I felt **ridiculous**. I couldn't quite explain it, but that's how it felt. Big parts of me were taken from me then. I was left with big holes in my being. It made me draw my little girl.

While doing EMDR, I experience **no kidding-dissociation**. Going through a memory from the church and the horror was about over, everything in me changed — my face, my posture, my voice, my

RIDICULES!

Sarah Hemli

feelings, and, in particular, my thoughts about the situation.

In a snap, the situation seemed far away. I had left the church and walked on the street with my dad, going home, probably still in physical pain. My little hand was in his big hand. **I was safe, I felt good, and I knew my dad would always be there for me to protect me.** My dad would never let anything bad happen to me!

My adult mind was flabbergasted. What just happened? How could a child even think that about the dad who had just given his daughter's body away to four men in one evening?

Processing another memory, from several months earlier, that I hadn't thought much about, I had a similar experience. After my dad had left the playhouse, it was **like I had woken from a deep sleep**. I had looked around the playhouse, wondering why my underwear was under the bench. Then I got dressed and walked down the little stairs, my red shoes at the bottom. The sun shone through leaves, and I wondering if my baby doll was still napping in the carriage outside of my playhouse. I checked, and she was.

The horror of what had just happened was erased from my mind!

These experiences helped me understand **how I survived**. It is how I could go on with my life as a child, how I made sense of it all. How I didn't go crazy. My mind had an amazing ability to **block out parts of my life that I didn't want to exist**.

Recalling the memory also showed me **which pain was more significant** to me as a child. Despite the physical pain and the emotional turmoil of what my dad did, in my young mind, I was sad he didn't play house with me after he said he would. I watched him walk away. Maybe he'd get things from the sandbox for us to have a pretend meal, but he passed it. He walked around the corner of the workshop. He'll be back, I thought, but **he never came back**. I was **crushed**.

It was hard to place my **anger** in the right spot. I was angry with **God** and with **myself**, with everyone but the one who deserved it. If I admitted what he really did, I'd expose myself to the world.

What if I was angry with my Far?

Sarah Hemli

HIJACKERS

MAYBE IT DIDN'T HAPPEN

GET IT RIGHT SOY GOOD

WHAT I THINK OTHERS THINK

WHAT IF I BELIEVED THE TRUE STUFF?

Over the week, I worked hard and so did Dahlia. I had **hope**. I had **peace**. I had dreams. **I wanted to go on living.**

I never remembered
BUT I always knew

Coming home to my life was hard. My relationship with Bruce was strained, partly because of the changes in me and partly because of choices he made in his life and of who he wanted to be. **It was difficult.**

I was trying **to hold on to me**, to not become invisible again. It was easy to fall back to familiar feelings of being stuck, helpless, and hopeless. I had to focus on the fact that

I chose my situation. I chose Bruce and I chose my kids and every day I chose to engage in life because of commitments I had made. So I was choosing to be stuck and I was not hopeless or helpless.

Dear little girl,

Things are different now. Back then you really were helpless. So many things were done to you and there was nothing you could do about it except to survive. You survived the hopelessness and the powerlessness. You made it through even though you had no choices.

Today we have choices, we are not helpless or without hope.

I know that at times it feels hopeless, but we are where we are because we chose to be...

...You know how I often just want to get away from it all, but I'm choosing to stay for my kids. They need their mom...

...just one more thing - Your dad was not a man of God. God was not for him or what he did. Little girl, God is good! He did not intend all this to happen to you, He wants what is good for you. He has put some really remarkable people around us. It's time for us to step out, to not be invisible anymore. Lets step out of the shadows and help make the world a better place for others.

Sarah

March 2014, translated from danish

Most of my struggles at this point were learning **to be fully me** and figuring out **who** that really was. **My past** was real, it was horrible, but it **didn't define me**.

The intrusive memories had stopped, my body had calmed, and flashbacks were fewer. **My marriage was in crisis**, but at the same time, it was a training ground for me to stay me and not let go and fall back to what I used to be — invisible.

I had opinions, likes, and dislikes. I was no longer willing to adapt to whatever Bruce

Sarah Hemli

wanted, or what he told me a good wife would be. I wasn't just an extension of him. **I wanted to be me**. I had changed, and I felt like it was somewhat unfair to Bruce. He had married a different person. He had said "I do" to a wife who existed to fulfill his needs. That was who I was. That was all I was. But now I wanted to be more, and Bruce was not happy to let go of his sweet deal.

So not only did I struggle internally, I **battled my husband for freedom** to be me. Often I would lose that battle. I'd try to stand up for myself, but I wore out quickly.

He'd **blame** me, put all of the responsibility on my shoulders, and I'd believe him. It **resonated** in me. The notion that I was bad and to blame for anything was deep and well rooted.

It's like I'm returning to some old coping strategies. Avoiding instead of standing up for myself, not following my food plan - either eating too much or not at all, wine, not wanting to be with friends, distracting myself. I'm not sure why now.

part of email to Dahlia April 2014

I can't do this. I just can't. I just went through 2 hours of bashing and I couldn't get out. I tried over and over again to find an out. None of those phrases that we've talked about worked. He just wouldn't let me go. Today has been awful - the birthday of misery. He got me a scented candle. I don't like scented candles, they smell fake. All I wanted was a new pitchfork and I kept hoping for it. But there was just nothing - no birthday, no cake, no dinner. The kids kept asking when we were gonna have cake, what I had asked for for my birthday dinner, when friends were coming over. Just nothing.
Tonight he topped it off with a threat to go file papers if I don't start working on our marriage.
I thought I could email you and sort out some of his words that way, but it's not working. It's just a mess, it's not working.

part of email to Dahlia May 2014

Bruce is gone this weekend so I've had time to ponder stuff. I've been think-ing about this all day - I can't think of a time in my life where I was more than just surviving. I've always had this sense of "I just have to get through another day" - but what's the purpose!?
Work, do stuff. My value is in what I can do. If I can get through the 20 things on my to do list, it's been a good day. I have no value just being.
I realized this as I was shovelling in the garden - maybe that's why I made a 1500 square feet garden, to make sure I never run out of work!
So I stopped, went and made a bonfire with the kids, they loved it.
What does it feel like to more than survive?

part of email to Dahlia May 2014

My old coping skills are so not working anymore. I try to fantasize but I can't hold on to the story, I get distracted. I try not to eat, it makes me feel good to see the numbers on the scale go down. It's not immediate though so it's not as effective.
So then I eat, it helps in the moment but then I get angry at myself for eating.
Then I do a ton of chores. I feel accomplished, but I still feel empty and angry.
Why am I so angry? Why am I just waiting for hours to go by. Why am I so aggravated?
This is not who I want to be!

from journal June 2014

Sarah Hemli

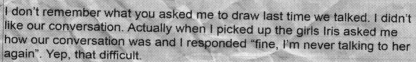

I don't remember what you asked me to draw last time we talked. I didn't like our conversation. Actually when I picked up the girls Iris asked me how our conversation was and I responded "fine, I'm never talking to her again". Yep, that difficult.

So anyways, I don't remember, but this is the picture in my head. Not sure what to say about it. It feels like I can't get to good and healthy things, I'm just stuck. I'm not sure what the walls of the box are made of, I wanted to put on 'hate, anger, disgust, pain' but it didn't seem quite right.

I've been so angry lately - out of control angry. Yesterday I was ok in the early morning, but when I found Matilda next to the chicken run screaming with a big "egg" on her forehead and found out that Mila and Grayson were throwing big rocks at the angry rooster and Matilda happened to take one for him - I just lost it. I yelled and sent them to their rooms, then went and yelled at them some more. I could not calm myself down and it really had nothing to do with rooster, rocks or kids. I went on the other side of the barn and screamed until my head hurt and my throat was sore. Later I was able to talk to the kids, apologize and lessen their consequences. But it was bad!

The rooster now limps. This is not who I want to be.

part of email to Dahlia June 2014

who I really am is who I am when I'm with Dahlia, Aaron or Grace or Iris - when I'm away from this place. I have joy, I have hope, I trust my memories, I have dreams, plans that I actually believe I can achieve. I have no compulsion to eat just to eat.

Then I come back home and I don't like who I am. I'm angry, I'm touchy, I'm easily offended, I feel hopeless and depressed. There's something about being in relationship with Bruce that takes me back to a younger version of me - a sad, blame taking, believing the crazy -me.

The real part of me fights against that and I become depressed and angry. I want to be able to be me all the time.

No wonder I don't like me here. I eat, and work and struggle. I wait for time to go by. I hate me.

from journal June 2014

Sarah Hemli

The past 2 days have been awful. It's happened again - it's like I've reverted into someone I don't want to be.
I've been depressed and angry. I've had no hope, no nothing. I've even had these strange dreams that I remember when I wake up in the morning.
I don't want to talk or be with anyone. When you cancelled today I was kind of relieved, I really didn't want to talk. What's the point? I thought about emailing you that I was done talking. I questioned your intentions anyways, Aaron and Grace's, Iris's. Thought about just going back to being here to fulfil Bruce's needs. Thought about not living at all.

I cannot see how all of this will ever turn out to be something good!
I've barely spoken to Bruce today. It makes him mad that I'm just ok all the time and he gets no details. Tonight at dinner Matilda asked loud and clear "why you cry mom when me nap? Please don't do that when me sleeping".
I knew Bruce's eyes were on me but I never looked at him. I felt like I was gonna get it. Him knowing that I had cried made me anxious.
He hasn't spoken to me since. He's kept in his room all evening.

It's so weird how this weekend I was really sad. My heart was so heavy when I stopped and allowed myself to feel it. But at the same time I could enjoy the kids. I had fun. I felt like things were gonna be ok somehow.
These past 2 days I've been really sad too but I'm just watching the minutes go by, trying to fill them so I'll make it through the day. And tomorrow is just another day that I have to survive.
I can see it. It's not how I want to live. But I don't know how to get back to a place of hope.
Sarah

part of email to Dahlia June 2014

God, I've been so angry with you. I hate what happened and I've blamed you for it. I can't be angry with him so I'm angry with you. You were there, you know everything that happened. You know how I've struggled through the years. So many years in this prison - walls made up of believing his definition of me. He defined who I was and what I was worth.

I've been so angry with you, I've rejected you for letting it all happen. You could have stopped him - or at least let me die

I'm sorry. I know you didn't intend this, it was his choice. He stopped me from being who you wanted me to be. What were your intentions for me? Who am I now?

I'm done living in his definition of me and his value of me.

Please forgive me! I don't really know you. I only know you through the eyes of overwhelming shame.

I want to know you. I want to know me. Who do you intend for me to be?

Please forgive me.

From journal June 2014

I had a flashback today while driving to pick up Nolan - something Matilda did brought it on, I think. I was angry and disappointed and trying to breathe and drive and push it away. I really didn't want it to be able to effect me that much anymore.

It had a different level of reality to it, well everything has had that the past few days - since we talked about whether my dad remembers or not and how he doesn't ask what's going on, coz he already knows. It's just an undeniable point that's hard to deal with.

The flashback is still echoing in my head, so sick of it.

part of email to Dahlia July 2014

I just realized - something has changed. Last week - I think - or maybe the week before I decided I was done being angry at and blaming God.

I still don't agree with him letting me live past 2 years old but angry just seemed pointless now.

I have no clue how to come close to him.

Sarah

part of email to Dahlia July 2014

So I know I'm gonna hear "how are you doing?" today at 1pm when we talk and I never know what to say. But today I was gonna have an answer for you, I was gonna figure it out this morning! So I sat down with my journal - quiet, calm, undisturbed... nothing!

I'm just ok, I'm nothing, I'm numb. I drew a picture. I'm ok, I'm managing to keep the top waters pretty calm but right under the surface is a storm of stuff. Talk to you later

part of email to Dahlia July 2014

More out of control anger coming up. I yelled in Bruce's face! It was like my body couldn't contain it. I was looking for things to hit or throw. I threw one of my most used kitchen bowls into the floor and it broke. I was screaming and slamming doors and stuff, but still I felt like I was gonna explode. (kids were all outside) My mind was going, "I don't want to live this, don't want to live." It began with kids - they keep removing rocks from the bottom of the chicken run fence = chickens everywhere. Then they come get me and tell me that somehow the chickens got out - completely innocent! I got angry and told them to go away from me. it's weird coz I felt like they were making a fool of me.

Then Bruce came home and got the worst of it - he does make me feel like a fool - asking me to have sex just coz he's been sober for 2 weeks. I yelled at him that I'm not a fool...

He began talking words, words, words about our relationship. How he's no longer looking at other women. He's made a lot of changes that I need to appreciate. And then he went on to explain to me that I'm a sexual being and I ought to want sex. He wanted to know if I masturbate?! He has the right to know those things because he is married to me.
I yelled that I hate all his words. I'm sick and tired of them. That he is not hearing me and if he could listen half as well as he can talk he could make a killing on that! He let me know how he understands that its easier for me to say that and "deflect" than to engage in the conversation.

He kept talking. Part of it was asking for forgiveness in a very nonchalant way. I responded "no, I can't forgive you". That's when fear kicked in. He said, "where does that leave us?" I added a "right now" and then I was done. Maybe I had gotten enough steam out to remember that I need to play it safe for my kids.
For about 30 minutes after that my stomach actually felt better than it has since Sunday.

part of email to Dahlia September 2014

Sarah Hemli

I struggled with **anger** and other emotions, in particular, **sorrow**. The more I accepted the truth, the more sad it became. **What a horrific life I had lived!** I was just a little girl depending on my parents to teach me about the world and how to live in it. Instead I learned how to survive the unthinkable. It impacted every fiber of my being. I was forever changed.

I finally had compassion for my younger self. It was so sad. But really anger was what came out of me again and again.

I was sitting peacefully on my bed one night writing to my little girl to figure out my food issues. I had already asked her about the anger and then I moved on to my weight, which led me to remember how my mom would hide chocolate in the freezer. I would sneak it. It was the first time in months a new memory came back, so I was quite surprised to be right back there, my dad behind me pressing me up against the deep freeze.

He steps back and says nothing, but **I know what to do**, he doesn't have to tell me. He says, in Danish, "**You bad girl. I can't believe you are asking your father to do this. You should be ashamed of yourself!**" He hits me and goes from there.

Interesting how different it was to have a new memory come up at this time in my journey. Had it been a year earlier, I would've resented myself: "See. She asked for it. She did it. It wasn't him. It was me. It's all my fault." But now **I understood the helplessness** I lived. My choices were to do what I needed to do, or object and make it worse.

My heart broke for my little girl who had to carry all this, not just what was done to her body but the overwhelming shame and the full **responsibility** for a grown man's evil choices. Hours later, it dawned on me that the memory was the answer to my anger.

As a mom, I'm held responsible for everything, from things lost, to the weather, and the speed of time. It seems there's no end to what I get blamed for. I react like that little girl who wasn't allowed to get angry or fight back. Such a great deal of responsibility and shame was put on me then, so that today, when someone tries to blame me for something that's not mine, **I explode!**

I've been writing to my little girl - makes me feel so crazy. I just don't understand the whole eating thing - what I'm avoiding or gaining or what ever. I didn't really find out. Part of a memory just keeps coming back.

I also wrote her about being so angry. I'm so sick of being angry, feeling like everyone is against me and blaming me for everything. It was really strange cos I continued to write about eating and stuff and then a new memory just hit me. I was really frustrated just for that. It wasn't until several hours later that it dawned on me that maybe what happened in that memory had something to do with my anger question.

So what if it does? I gotta get rid of this anger. It just jumps out at every little irritation and it's not like I have time to think - I just react - overreact that is! This past week I left Matilda alone downstairs for a little. When I came back, she had soaked the office chair seat in hand sanitizer and put hair wax in her own hair and on 2 cats! I got so mad!

I told my friend about it later and she just laughed - Matilda is breaking in the cats! My friend was right; it was funny. Sure, Matilda should have sat in timeout and been told how that's not ok, but my anger was out of proportions.

I really gotta figure this out.

part of email to Dahlia September 2014

Dear little girl,

Are you angry? I feel this overwhelming anger come out of me. Are you angry? You have a lot of reasons, it's not that. So much was taking from you when you were so little and helpless. There's much to be angry about, but we have to find a better way to get it out.

Tell me what you are angry about!

Everything changed back then. what he did changed who we are forever. His choices defined us from then on. It has affected us for so many years. It's been right under the surface - invisible - but its bled out to every aspect of our life. Life has been a battle, only survival, exhausting cover up work to keep everything hidden.

what happened happened, he did what he did, but he's not gonna have anymore control in our life. You have to let go of the anger. You have to let go of his control. we are in control now.

Sarah

from journal September 2014, translated from danish

Sarah Hemli

It's time to give the responsibility, the shame, the blame to the one it rightfully belongs to.

That's **my dad's house.** The dream house we called it. I helped him build it. For two summers I "worked" for him building his house. Those were good times. He taught me a lot about building. He's not all bad, but **this rubble belongs to him**.

After I drew it, I wondered if I should have put a front loader or a pickup truck in the drawing, but no, a hand truck is the right thing.

It's been time consuming, hands on, **hard work** to get this rubble off of me and moved to its rightful owner.

It's quite a mess there in front of his house. It's not pretty, but **for the first time ever, it's not my mess**.

What my dad did to me **no longer defines me. It defines him. I get to define myself!**

I'm **keeping a few pieces of rubble**. I'm keeping some to remind me of my **strength** and **will to survive**. I'm keeping those that make me a person of compassion, empathy, and understanding. I'm keeping some to remember **life is hard** and everyone has their own rubble to deal with.

I struggled with God. I didn't know how to make peace with Him. It seemed like an ever-returning **battle** and not one that could be settled. I didn't get it. I felt unable to relate to him in any way. The God who trusted me to my dad, who knew everything that went on, who could have let me die or not be born. The God who could have stopped my dad but didn't.

How could I trust this God?!

Sarah Hemli

My dad was close to God. They spent time together morning and evening. God was number one for my dad. He'd pray often, read the Word, and worship. **Jesus died for my dad**. He gave his life for my dad in spite of what he did, in spite of there being **no remorse**, **no repentance** — at least not expressed toward me.

My dad lived with the assurance that the things he had done were forgiven by God. So much so that he could just forget about it. Meanwhile, I was the victim, but I had lived with his sin my whole life. I had gone through agony, while my dad got to forget it.

How was I supposed to connect to that same God?

The God who was right there in my room leaning up against my toddler bed was **crying**.

What good was crying? It made me so angry. The Almighty Maker of the Universe was crying, instead of doing something. It made him sad, but not sad enough to actually step in?

I always came back to the same question —

why let me live?

At the same time, I knew God was the one who gave my growing mind the **ability to disassociate** from the horrific things that happened to me. He provided for my **means of survival**, to simply set aside what was happening so I could function as a normal child.

In my head, I saw this picture while Aaron was praying with me the last time we were together in North Carolina. I saw myself in my tree house and I saw **God's hands holding my head**. God was there. He didn't stop what was happening. He didn't change the situation. He held my mind. It didn't break. I didn't develop a personality disorder. I didn't go crazy. **I was in His hands**.

My mind kept it all contained for so many years until **God brought the right**

people along for me to work through it.

Over the past two years of my life, how many times have I wondered why?

For years I **asked God to let me remember**. I struggled with knowing that something happened but not remembering. I was frustrated. But really, had I known how hard it would be to get through it, I **would've settled for frustrated**.

I was doing a lot better at this point. Although I could still easily be pushed to a numb or hopeless state, it seemed to be for shorter durations until I'd snap back and move forward again.

I felt **more aware** of my reactions, my anxiety, how different situations affected me. It seemed odd to have done so much work to heal and then be more sensitive to the world around me. At a glance, it was **easier to**

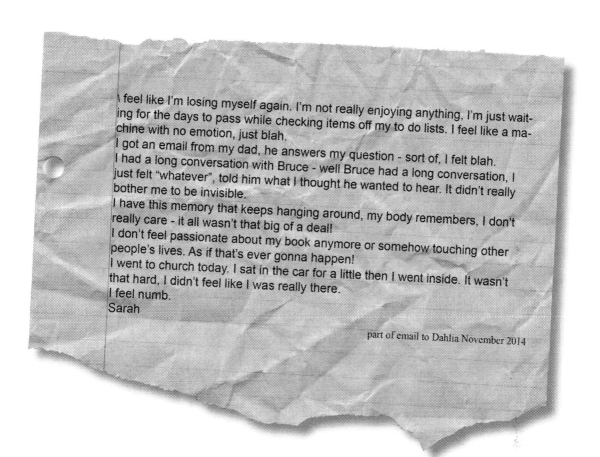

I feel like I'm losing myself again. I'm not really enjoying anything, I'm just waiting for the days to pass while checking items off my to do lists. I feel like a machine with no emotion, just blah.
I got an email from my dad, he answers my question - sort of, I felt blah.
I had a long conversation with Bruce - well Bruce had a long conversation, I just felt "whatever", told him what I thought he wanted to hear. It didn't really bother me to be invisible.
I have this memory that keeps hanging around, my body remembers, I don't really care - it all wasn't that big of a deal!
I don't feel passionate about my book anymore or somehow touching other people's lives. As if that's ever gonna happen!
I went to church today. I sat in the car for a little then I went inside. It wasn't that hard, I didn't feel like I was really there.
I feel numb.
Sarah

part of email to Dahlia November 2014

navigate the world numb.

Church was particularly difficult.

Can you love God and hate church? I didn't know if I'd ever be able to make peace with the concept of church.

I went for my kids. I wanted them to enjoy Christian fellowship and belonging. But I felt like a hypocrite. As soon as I entered the building, my hypervigilance kicked into high gear. My **body was as tight as a knot**. I fought **tears**. I could smile and say Hi, but don't be fooled, I was ready to claw out eyes if anyone came too close.

The **biggest challenge was the pastors**. I had completely written off one of them, I had never spoken to him. I knew nothing about him and I didn't plan to. But there was something about the other that made me want to **give him a chance**. Something that made me think he might be **trustworthy**. I spoke to him, shared my story with him, he still didn't feel safe. I watched him to make sure I knew where he was. I liked it best when he was in the pulpit teaching and everyone was watching him. That's when I found the guts to enter the sanctuary. **Some Sundays I never made it** in there.

I told myself these **people were okay**. They didn't do anything to me.

They couldn't hurt me, but **my body disregarded logical thinking**. It remembered as clear as yesterday being abused by strange men while other male **voices sang praise songs** in the sanctuary.

I tried to do the church thing for a long time. I thought maybe it would get better, but it never did. In fact, it got harder. I reacted so strongly that if God was there, I would not have been able to meet Him anyways. **I would have to find God in different places**.

I gave up on church, blaming it on the pastor and people. It was easier to blame others than admit it was too hard for me. I didn't go for several months until my kids began asking to go again. I gave it another try which just ended in **another defeat**.

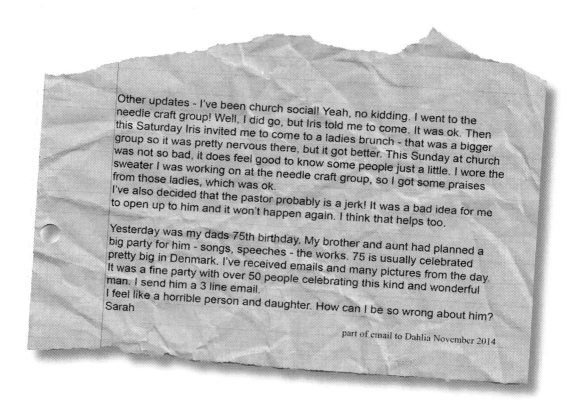

Other updates - I've been church social! Yeah, no kidding. I went to the needle craft group! Well, I did go, but Iris told me to come. It was ok. Then this Saturday Iris invited me to come to a ladies brunch - that was a bigger group so it was pretty nervous there, but it got better. This Sunday at church was not so bad, it does feel good to know some people just a little. I wore the sweater I was working on at the needle craft group, so I got some praises from those ladies, which was ok.
I've also decided that the pastor probably is a jerk! It was a bad idea for me to open up to him and it won't happen again. I think that helps too.

Yesterday was my dads 75th birthday. My brother and aunt had planned a big party for him - songs, speeches - the works. 75 is usually celebrated pretty big in Denmark. I've received emails and many pictures from the day. It was a fine party with over 50 people celebrating this kind and wonderful man. I send him a 3 line email.
I feel like a horrible person and daughter. How can I be so wrong about him?
Sarah

part of email to Dahlia November 2014

Sarah Hemli

In spite of my anxiety, I had come a long way in my journey that would continue for the rest of my life.

Things were **different**. I was different. My **marriage was in shambles**. I had **lost the connection with my parents**. I still had questions. I **battled myself. Battled God**. I reacted too emotionally. **But I had me**. I had **value**. I had purpose and place in this world. I had choices!

I never remembered but I always knew. For years I had made choices based upon my past. Big or small, all decisions had come from that place of no value, no importance, only worth in what I could do for others. I had been lost.

I hadn't had memories to connect to, **living the symptoms of my childhood everyday** as I made my way through life believing I deserved nothing good. **I had survived**.

Today I'm able to make choices based on **who I am** — my **values**, my **beliefs**. I am somebody! **I'm important** enough to the Maker of the Universe for Him to sit on the floor of my toddler bedroom. **He shed tears for the pain I had to live**. I matter that much to Him. He kept it all hidden in my mind until He carefully wove together the past two years of my life so I could **work** through this and **find myself**.

He put **people** in my life to walk this road with me. My friend across the Atlantic knew Aaron, who knew Dahlia. Somehow I found the courage to trust them, and they helped me open the door to so much rubble. He gave me new parents in Aaron and Grace. He gave me a few local friendships I could really rely on. **He put everything in place for me** to work through my past.

I see **His hand** in it all. He began it and walked with me through it. Still I doubt Him at times. I question Him. There are so many questions.

I want to believe **He is a good God all the time**. I want to believe He is **always for me**. I want to believe He will **use it all for good**. I want to trust Him, **I want to love Him**.

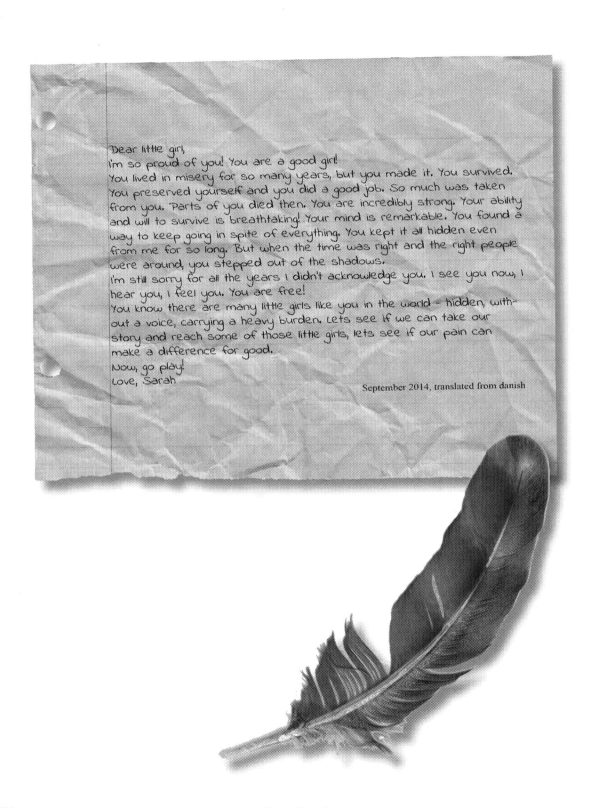

Dear little girl,
I'm so proud of you! You are a good girl!
You lived in misery for so many years, but you made it. You survived.
You preserved yourself and you did a good job. So much was taken
from you. Parts of you died then. You are incredibly strong. Your ability
and will to survive is breathtaking! Your mind is remarkable. You found a
way to keep going in spite of everything. You kept it all hidden even
from me for so long. But when the time was right and the right people
were around, you stepped out of the shadows.
I'm still sorry for all the years I didn't acknowledge you. I see you now, I
hear you, I feel you. You are free!
You know there are many little girls like you in the world – hidden, without a voice, carrying a heavy burden. Lets see if we can take our
story and reach some of those little girls, lets see if our pain can
make a difference for good.
Now, go play!
Love, Sarah

September 2014, translated from danish

Sarah Hemli

I will keep walking.

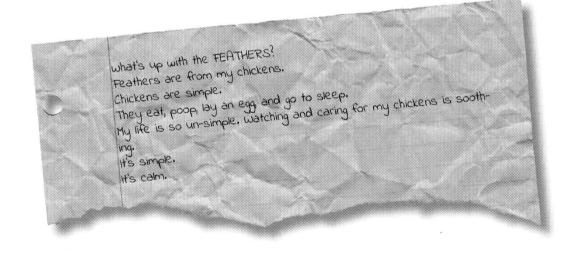

What's up with the FEATHERS?
Feathers are from my chickens.
Chickens are simple.
They eat, poop, lay an egg and go to sleep.
My life is so un-simple. Watching and caring for my chickens is sooth-
ing.
It's simple.
It's calm.

Sarah Hemli

Printed in the United States
By Bookmasters